Recent Photo of the Author

佛法無邊

法輪常轉

This Falun emblem is the miniature of the universe.
It also has its own form of existence and process of
evolution in all other dimensions; therefore, I call
it a world.

Li Hongzhi

FALUN GONG
(REVISED EDITION)

(ENGLISH VERSION)

LI HONGZHI

FAIR WINDS
PRESS

GLOUCESTER, MASSACHUSETTES

Published in the United States of America by
Fair Winds Press
33 Commercial Street
Gloucester, Massachusetts 01930-5089

ISBN 1-931412-61-8

10 9 8 7 6 5 4 3 2 1

Cover Design: Linda Kosarin

Printed in Canada

LUNYU[1]

The BUDDHA FA[2] is most profound; it is the most intricate and extraordinary science of all theories in the world. In order to explore this domain, people must fundamentally change their conventional human notions. Failing that, the truth of the universe will forever remain a mystery to humankind, and everyday people will forever crawl within the boundaries set by their own ignorance.

So what exactly is this BUDDHA FA, then? A religion? A philosophy? It is understood as such only by "modernized scholars of Buddhism." They merely study it on a theoretical level, regarding it as something that falls within the domain of philosophy for critical studies and so-called research. In actuality, the BUDDHA FA is not limited to the little portion in the sutras, which is only the BUDDHA FA at an elementary level. From particles and molecules to the universe, from the even smaller to the even greater, the BUDDHA FA offers insight into all mysteries, encompassing everything and omitting nothing. It is the nature of the universe, Zhen-Shan-Ren,[3] expressed in different ways at different levels. It is also what the Dao School calls the Dao,[4] and what the Buddha School calls the Fa.

No matter how advanced the science of today's humankind may be, it can only account for part of the universe's mys-

---

[1] Lunyu (loon-yew)—"An explanation using language."

[2] Fa (fah)—"Law," "Way," or "Principles."

[3] Zhen-Shan-Ren (juhn-shahn-ren)—Zhen means "truth, truthfulness"; Shan, "benevolence, compassion, kindness"; Ren, "forbearance, tolerance, endurance, self-control."

[4] Dao (dow)—"the Way" (also spelled "Tao").

teries. Once we mention specific phenomena of the BUDDHA FA, there are people who will say: "We're now in the electronic age, and science is so advanced. Spaceships have flown to other planets, but you're still talking about these old superstitions." To be frank, no matter how advanced computers may be, they are no match for the human brain, which remains an enigma to this day. Regardless of how far spaceships may travel, they still cannot fly beyond this physical dimension in which our human race exists. What can be understood with today's human knowledge is still extremely shallow and limited—it is nowhere near a genuine understanding of the true nature of the universe. Some people do not even dare to face up to, approach, or acknowledge the facts of phenomena that objectively exist, all because these people are too conservative and are unwilling to change their conventional notions when thinking. Only the BUDDHA FA can completely unveil the mysteries of the universe, space-time, and the human body. It can truly distinguish the kind from the wicked, the good from the bad, and it can dispel all misconceptions while providing a correct understanding of things.

The guiding principles of today's human science confine its development and research to this physical world, as a subject will not be studied until it is acknowledged—it follows this path. As for phenomena that are intangible and invisible, but objectively existing and reflected into our physical world as real manifestations, they are avoided and treated as inexplicable phenomena. Stubborn people have, on unsubstantiated grounds, entrenched themselves in their argument that these are just "natural" phenomena. People with ulterior motives have acted against their own consciences by labeling all of these phenomena as superstitions. People with unprobing minds have shied away from these matters with the excuse that science is not sufficiently advanced to deal with them. Humankind will make a leap forward if it can take a fresh look at itself and the universe, changing its rigid mindset. The BUDDHA FA can provide people with insight into immeasurable and boundless worlds. Throughout the ages, only the BUDDHA FA has been able to completely explain human beings, the various dimensions of material existence, life, and the entire universe.

Contents

Chapter I
Introduction

In our country, [China], *qigong¹* has a long history, as it dates back to ancient times. Our people thus have a natural advantage in practicing *qigong*. The two upright schools of *qigong* cultivation practice, the Buddha School and the Dao School, have already made public many great cultivation methods previously taught in private. The Dao School's ways of cultivation are quite unique, while the Buddha School has its own cultivation methods. Falun Gong² is an advanced cultivation method of the Buddha School. In this lecture series, I will first adjust your body to a state suitable for advanced cultivation and then install a Falun³ and energy mechanisms (*qiji*) in your body. I will also teach you our exercises. In addition to all of these things, I have Law Bodies (*fashen*) who will protect you. But your having only these things is inadequate, as they can't achieve the goal of developing *gong⁴*—it's necessary that you also understand the principles for cultivation at high levels. That is what this book will address.

I am teaching the practice system at high levels, so I won't discuss cultivation of any particular meridian,⁵ acupuncture point, or energy passage. I am teaching a great cultivation way, the great way for true cultivation to high levels. Initially it might sound inconceivable. But as

---

¹ *qigong* (chee-gong)—a general name for certain practices that cultivate the human body. In recent decades, *qigong* exercises have been incredibly popular in China.

² Falun Gong (fah-lun gong)—"Law Wheel Qigong." The names Falun Gong and Falun Dafa are both used to refer to this practice.

³ Falun (fah-lun)—"Law Wheel" (see color page at front).

⁴ *gong* (gong)—"cultivation energy."

1

long as those who are dedicated to practicing *qigong* carefully explore and experience the practice, they will find all the wonders and intricacies within it.

1. The Origins of Qigong

The *qigong* that we refer to today was not, in fact, originally called *qigong*. It originated from the solitary cultivation ways of the ancient Chinese people and from cultivation in religions. The two-character term, *qi gong*, is nowhere to be found in the texts *Scripture of Dan Cultivation*, the *Daoist Canon*,[6] or the *Tripitaka*.[7] During the course of our present human civilization's development, *qigong* passed through the period when religions were in their embryonic forms. It had already existed before religions came into being. After religions formed, it acquired some degree of religious overtones. *Qigong's* original names were The Great Cultivation Way of Buddha, and The Great Cultivation Way of Dao. It had other names, such as Nine-fold Internal Alchemy, The Way of Arhat,[8] The Dhyana of Vajra,[9] etc. We now call it *qigong* so that it better suits our modern thinking and is more easily popularized in society. *Qigong* is actually something existing in China for the sole purpose of cultivating the human body.

---

[5] meridian—the network of energy channels in one's body that are thought to be conduits of *qi*. In Traditional Chinese Medicine and popular Chinese thought, illness is said to arise when *qi* is not flowing properly through these meridians.

[6] *Scripture of Dan Cultivation* (dahn), *Daoist Canon*—ancient, classic Chinese Daoist texts for practicing cultivation.

[7] *Tripitaka*—"The Three Baskets," also known as the Pali Canon. This is a collection of primary Pali-language texts that form the doctrinal foundation of Theravada Buddhism. Its three parts are: teachings of the Buddha, the monastic code, and special philosophical treatises.

Qigong is not something invented by this civilization. It has a fairly long history that dates back to distant years. So, when did *qigong* come into being? Some say that *qigong* has a history of three thousand years, and became quite popular during the Tang Dynasty.[10] Some say it has a history of five thousand years and is as old as Chinese civilization. Some say that, judging from archaeological findings, it has a history of seven thousand years thus far. I regard *qigong* as something not invented by modern humankind—it is from prehistoric culture. According to investigation by people with supernormal abilities, the universe we live in is an entity that was remade after being exploded nine times. The planet we dwell on has been destroyed many times. Each time the planet was remade, humankind again began to multiply. At present, we have already discovered that there are many things on the earth that surpass our present civilization. According to Darwin's theory of evolution, humans evolved from apes, and civilization is no more than ten thousand years old. Yet archaeological findings have revealed that in the caves of the European Alps there exist 250-thousand-year-old frescoes that exhibit a very high level of artistry—one far beyond the abilities of modern people. In the museum of the National University of Peru, there is a large rock on which is an engraved figure who holds a telescope and is observing the stars. This figure is more than thirty thousand years old. As we know, Galileo invented a 30X astronomical telescope in 1609, just over three hundred years ago. How could there have been a telescope thirty thousand years ago? There is an iron pillar in India whose iron content is over

---

[8] Arhat—enlightened being with Attainment Status in the Buddha School who is beyond the Triple World but lower than Bodhisattva.

[9] Dhyana of Vajra—Dhyana translates as "Meditation," while Vajra can be translated as "Thunderbolt," "Diamond," or "Indestructible."

[10] Tang (tahng) Dynasty—one of the most prosperous periods in Chinese history (618 - 907 A.D.).

ninety-nine percent. Even modern smelting technology cannot produce iron with such high purity; it had already surpassed the level of modern technology. Who created those civilizations? How could human beings—who would have been microorganisms in those times—have created these things? These discoveries have caught the attention of scientists worldwide. They are considered to be from prehistoric culture since they prove inexplicable.

The level of scientific achievement was different in each time period. In some time periods it was quite high, surpassing that of our modern humankind. But those civilizations were destroyed. Therefore, I say that *qigong* wasn't invented or created by modern people, but discovered and perfected by modern people. It is from prehistoric culture.

Qigong is not exclusively a product of our country. It exists in foreign countries as well, but they don't call it *qigong*. Western countries, such as the United States, Great Britain, etc., call it magic. David Copperfield, a magician in the US, is a master of supernormal abilities who once performed the feat of walking through the Great Wall of China. When he was about to pass through the Wall, he used a white cloth as a cover, pressed himself against the Wall, and then proceeded to go through it. Why did he do that? Doing it that way would lead many people to consider it a magic show. It had to be done like that since he knew there are many people in China with great supernormal abilities. He was afraid of interference from them, so he covered himself before he went in. When coming out, he raised the cloth with one hand and walked out. As the saying goes, "Experts watch for tricks while laymen watch for excitement." With it done this way the audience thought it was a magic performance. These supernormal abilities are called magic because they aren't used for cultivating the human body, but for stage performances in order to display unusual things and to entertain. From a low-level perspective,

4

qigong can change the condition of one's body, achieving the goals of healing and health. From a high-level perspective, *qigong* refers to the cultivation of one's original-body (*benti*).

2. Qi and Gong

The *qi*[11] we now talk about was called *chee*[12] by ancient people. They are essentially the same, as both refer to the *qi* of the universe—a shapeless, invisible kind of substance existing throughout the universe. *Qi* does not refer to air. The energy of this substance is activated in the human body through practicing cultivation. Its activation changes the body's physical condition and can have the effect of producing healing and health. Yet *qi* is merely *qi*—you have *qi*, he has *qi*, and one person's *qi* cannot have a restraining effect on another's *qi*. Some say that *qi* can cure illnesses, or that you can emit *qi* toward someone to cure his or her illness. These remarks are rather unscientific, as *qi* cannot cure illness in the least. When a practitioner's body still contains *qi*, it means that his or her body is not yet a Milk-White Body. That is, the practitioner still carries illness.

A person who obtains advanced abilities through cultivation does not emit *qi*. Instead, he or she emits a cluster of high energy. It is a high-energy substance that manifests in the form of light, and its particles are fine and its density is high. This is *gong*. Only this can have a restraining effect on everyday people, and only with this can one treat sicknesses for others. There is a saying,

---

[11] *qi* (chee)—in Chinese thought, this substance/energy is said to assume many forms in the body and the environment. Usually translated as "vital energy," this *qi* is thought to determine a person's health.

[12] This term uses a different Chinese character than *qi*, but is pronounced the same way.

5

"A Buddha's light shines everywhere and rectifies all abnormalities." It means that those who practice true cultivation carry immense energy in their bodies. Wherever these persons go, any abnormal condition within the area covered by their energy can be corrected and restored to normal. For instance, sickness in one's body is truly an abnormal bodily state, and the sickness will disappear after this state is corrected. More simply put, *gong* is energy. *Gong* has physical characteristics, and practitioners can experience and perceive its objective existence through practicing cultivation.

3. Gong Potency and Supernormal Abilities

(1) Gong Potency is Developed Through Cultivating Xinxing[13]

The *gong* that truly determines the level of one's *gong* potency (*gongli*) isn't developed through performing *qigong* exercises. It is developed through the transformation of the substance called virtue (*de*), and through the cultivation of *xinxing*. This transformation process isn't accomplished by "setting up a crucible and furnace to make an elixir from gathered chemicals,"[14] as imagined by everyday people. The *gong* we refer to is generated outside the body, and it begins at the lower half of the body. Following the improvement of one's *xinxing,* it grows upward in a spiral shape and forms completely outside one's body. Upon reaching the crown of the head it then develops into a *gong* column. The height of this *gong* column determines the level of a

---

[13] *xinxing* (shin-shing)—"mind nature" or "heart nature"; "moral character."

[14] In the Daoist tradition, external alchemical processes have long served as metaphors to describe internal cultivation of the human body.

person's *gong*. The *gong* column exists in a deeply hidden dimension, making it difficult for an average person to see it.

Supernormal abilities are strengthened by *gong* potency. The higher a person's *gong* potency and level, the greater his or her supernormal abilities are and the easier they are to use. People with lower *gong* potency have weaker supernormal abilities; they find it harder to use them, and some are completely unusable. Supernormal abilities themselves represent neither the level of one's *gong* potency nor the level of one's cultivation. What determines one's level is *gong* potency, rather than supernormal abilities. Some people cultivate in a "locked" mode, whereby their *gong* potency is rather high but they don't necessarily possess many supernormal abilities. *Gong* potency is the determining factor, is developed through *xinxing* cultivation, and is the most crucial thing.

(2) Supernormal Abilities are Not What Cultivators Pursue

All practitioners care about supernormal abilities. Supernatural abilities are attractive to the general public and many people want to acquire some. Yet without good *xinxing* one won't be able to acquire supernormal abilities.

Some supernormal abilities that might be possessed by everyday people include an open Third Eye[15] (*tianmu*), clairaudience, telepathy, precognition, etc. But not all of these supernormal abilities will appear during the stages of Gradual Enlightenment, as they vary with each individual. It is impossible

---

[15] Third Eye—sometimes translated as "Celestial Eye," this term (*tianmu*) is used flexibly and can refer to the Third Eye system or a particular component of that system.

for everyday people to have certain supernormal abilities, such as that of transforming one kind of substance in this physical dimension into another kind of substance—this isn't something everyday people can have. Great supernormal abilities are only developed through cultivating after birth. Falun Gong was developed based on the principles of the universe, so all supernormal abilities that exist in the universe exist in Falun Gong. It all depends on how a practitioner cultivates. The thought of acquiring some supernormal abilities isn't considered wrong. Nevertheless, excessively intense pursuit is more than a normal thought and will produce negative results. It is of little use for someone at a low level to acquire supernormal abilities, save for trying to employ these to show off his or her abilities in front of everyday people and hoping to become the stronger one among them. If this is the case, it indicates precisely that the person's *xinxing* is not high and that it is right not to give him or her supernormal abilities. Some supernormal abilities can be used to commit wrongdoing if they are given to people with poor *xinxing*. Because those people's *xinxing* are not steady there is no guarantee that they won't do something bad.

On the other hand, any supernormal abilities that can be demonstrated or performed cannot change human society or alter normal social life. Real high-level supernormal abilities are not allowed to be brought out for show, because the impact and danger would be too great; for example, one would never perform the pulling down of a large building. Great supernormal abilities are not allowed to be used except by people with special missions, and neither can these abilities be revealed; this is because high-level masters restrain them.

All the same, some everyday people insist on having *qigong* masters perform, forcing them to display their supernormal abilities. People with supernormal abilities are unwilling to use them for performance, since they are forbidden to reveal them; displaying them would impact the entire state of society. People who genuinely possess great virtue are not allowed to use their supernormal abilities in public. Some *qigong* masters feel awful during performances and want to cry afterward. Don't force them to perform! It is upsetting to them to reveal these things. A student brought a magazine to me. I felt disgusted the moment I read it. It mentioned that an international *qigong* conference was to be held. People with supernormal abilities could participate in a contest, and the conference was open to whoever had great supernormal abilities. After I read it I felt upset for days. Supernormal abilities are not something that can be publicly displayed for competition—demonstrating them in public is regrettable. Everyday people focus on practical things in the mundane world, but *qigong* masters need to have dignity.

What's the motive behind wanting supernormal abilities? Wanting them reflects a practitioner's realm of mind and pursuits. A person with impure pursuits and an unstable mind is unlikely to have great supernormal abilities. This is because before you are fully enlightened, what you perceive to be good or bad is only based on the standards of this world. You can see neither the true nature of things nor the karmic relationships among them. Fighting, cursing, and mistreatment among people are inherently caused by karmic relationships. You can only be more trouble than help if you can't perceive them. The gratitude and resentment, right and wrong of everyday people are governed by the laws of this world; practitioners shouldn't be concerned with these things. Before you achieve full Enlightenment, what you see with your eyes might not necessarily be the truth. When one person punches another, it might be that they are settling their karmic debts. Your involvement might hamper the settlement of the debt. Karma is a type of black substance that surrounds the human body. It has physical existence in another dimension and can transform into sickness or misfortune.

Supernormal abilities exist in everyone, and the idea is that they need to be developed and strengthened through continued cultivation. If, as a practitioner, a person only pursues supernormal abilities, he is shortsighted and impure in mind. No matter what he wants supernormal abilities for, his pursuit contains elements of selfishness that will definitely hinder cultivation. Consequently, he will never obtain supernormal abilities.

(3) Handling Gong Potency

Some practitioners haven't practiced for very long, yet they want to treat illnesses for others to see how effective they are. When those of you without high *gong* potency extend your hand and try, you absorb into your own body a great deal of black, unhealthy, filthy *qi* that exists in the patient's body. Since you don't have the ability to resist unhealthy *qi* and your body also lacks a protective shield, you form one shared field with the patient; you can't defend against unhealthy *qi* without high *gong* potency. As a result, you will experience a great deal of discomfort. If no one looks after you, over the course of time you will accumulate illness throughout your body. So someone who lacks high *gong* potency shouldn't treat illnesses for others. Only a person who has already developed supernormal abilities and who possesses a certain level of *gong* potency can use *qigong* to treat illness. Even though some people have developed supernormal abilities and are able to treat illnesses, they are, when at a rather low level, in fact using their accumulated *gong* potency—their own energy—to treat the illnesses. Since *gong* is both energy and an intelligent entity that isn't easily accumulated, you are actually depleting yourself of *gong* when you emit it. Accompanying your release of *gong*, the *gong* column above your head shortens and depletes. That is not worth it at all. So I don't endorse treating illness for others when your *gong* potency is not high. No matter how great the methods you used, you would still consume your own energy.

All kinds of supernormal abilities will emerge when a person's *gong* potency reaches a certain level. You need to be very cautious when using these supernormal abilities. For instance, a person has to use his Third Eye once it has opened, as it will close if he never uses it. Yet he shouldn't look through it frequently. Too much energy will be discharged if he looks through it too often. So does this mean one should never use it? Of course not. If we were to never use it, then what would be the use of our practicing cultivation? The question is when to use it. You can use it only when you have cultivated to a certain stage and possess the ability to replenish yourself. When a cultivator of Falun Gong reaches a certain stage, the Falun can automatically transform and replenish however much *gong* he or she releases. The Falun automatically maintains a practitioner's *gong* potency level, and his or her *gong* won't decrease for even one moment. This is a characteristic of Falun Gong. Not until that point may supernormal abilities be used.

4. The Third Eye

(1) Opening the Third Eye

The Third Eye's main passage is located between the middle of the forehead and the Shangen[16] point. The way everyday people see things with the naked eye works the same way as a camera does: The size of the lens, or pupil, is adjusted according to the distance of an object and the intensity of the light. Via the optic

---

[16] Shangen (shahn-gun) point—acupuncture point located between one's eyebrows and slightly below.

nerves, images then form on the pineal gland, located at the back of the brain. The supernormal ability of Penetrative Vision is simply the ability of the pineal gland to look directly out through the Third Eye. An average person's Third Eye is closed, as his or her main passage is narrow and dark. There is no quintessential *qi* inside, no illumination. Some people cannot see, for their passages are blocked.

To open the Third Eye, we first use either outside force or self-cultivation to unblock the passage. The shape of the passage varies with each individual, ranging from oval to round, rhombic to triangular. The better you cultivate, the rounder the passage will become. Second, the master gives you an eye. If you cultivate on your own then you have to cultivate it yourself. Third, you need to have quintessential *qi*[17] at the location of your Third Eye.

We usually see things with our two eyes, and it is exactly these two eyes that block our channel to other dimensions. Since they function as a shield, we can only see objects that exist in our physical dimension. Opening the Third Eye allows you to see without using these two eyes. You can also cultivate to have a True Eye after you reach a very high level. Then you can see with the True Eye of The Third Eye, or with the True Eye at the Shangen point. According to the Buddha School, every pore of the body is an eye—there are eyes all over the body. According to the Dao School, every acupuncture point is an eye. The main passage is nonetheless located at the Third Eye, and it has to be

---

[17] *"Qi"* can also be used in a much broader sense to describe substances that are invisible and amorphous, such as air, smell, anger, etc.

[18] Master—the Chinese term used here, *shifu*, is composed of two characters: one meaning "teacher," the other "father."

opened first. In class, I plant in everyone things that can open the Third Eye. The results vary owing to differences in people's physical qualities. Some people see a dark hole similar to a deep well. This means the passage of the Third Eye is dark. Others see a white tunnel. If objects can be seen in front, the Third Eye is about to open. Some see objects revolving, which are what Master[18] has planted to open the Third Eye. You will be able to see once the Third Eye is drilled open. Some people can see a large eye through their Third Eye, and they think it is the Buddha's eye. It is actually their own eye. These are usually people with relatively good inborn quality.

According to our statistics, the Third Eye is opened for more than half of the attendees each time we give a lecture series. A problem might arise after the Third Eye is opened, wherein a person whose *xinxing* isn't high can easily use the Third Eye to do bad things. To prevent this problem, I open your Third Eye directly to the level of Wisdom Eyesight—in other words, to an advanced level that allows you to directly see scenes from other dimensions and to see things that appear during cultivation, allowing you to believe them. This will reinforce your confidence in cultivation. The *xinxing* of people who have just started practicing have not yet reached the level of supernormal people. They are thus inclined to do wrong once they possess supernormal things. Let's give a playful example: If you were to walk along the street and come upon a lottery stand, you might be able to walk away with the first prize. This won't be allowed to happen— it's just to illustrate the point. Another reason is that we are opening the Third Eye for a large number of people. Suppose every person's Third Eye was opened at a lower level: Just imagine if everyone could see through the human body or see objects behind walls—could we still call this a human society? Human society would be severely disrupted, so it is neither permissible nor achievable. Furthermore, it wouldn't do practitioners any good and would only foster their attachments. So we won't open the Third Eye for you at a low level. We will instead open it directly at a high level.

(2) The Third Eye's Levels

The Third Eye has many different levels; at different levels it sees different dimensions. According to Buddhism there are five levels: Flesh Eyesight, Celestial Eyesight, Wisdom Eyesight, Law Eyesight, and Buddha Eyesight. Each level is subdivided into upper, middle, and lower levels. Only our material world can be observed when at or below the level of Celestial Eyesight. Only at or above the level of Wisdom Eyesight will other dimensions be observable. Those who have the supernormal ability of Penetrative Vision can see things accurately, with clarity better than that of a CAT scan. But what they can see is still within this physical world and doesn't exceed the dimension in which we exist; they aren't considered to have reached an advanced level of the Third Eye.

The level of a person's Third Eye is determined by the amount of his or her quintessential *qi*, as well as the width, brightness, and degree of blockage of the main passage. The internal, quintessential *qi* is critical in determining how thoroughly the Third Eye will be able to open. It is particularly easy to open the Third Eye for children under the age of six. I needn't even bother using my hand, as it opens once I start talking. This is because children have received little negative influence from our physical world and they haven't committed any wrongdoing. Their quintessential *qi* is well preserved. The Third Eye of a child over the age of six becomes increasingly difficult to open, owing to the increase of external influences as they grow up. In particular,

14

unsound education, being spoiled, and turning immoral can all make the quintessential *qi* dissipate. All of it will be gone after a certain point is reached. Those people whose quintessential *qi* is completely lost can gradually recover it through cultivation, but it takes a long period of time and arduous effort. So the quintessential *qi* is extremely precious.

I don't recommend that a person's Third Eye be opened at the level of Celestial Eyesight, because a practitioner with low *gong* potency will lose more energy looking at objects than he accumulates through cultivation. The Third Eye might once again close if too much of the essential energy is lost. Once it closes it won't be easy to open again. So I usually open the Third Eye for people at the level of Wisdom Eyesight. No matter how clear or unclear a cultivator's vision is, he or she will be able to see objects in other dimensions. Since people are affected by their innate qualities, some see clearly, some see things intermittently, and others see unclearly. But at a minimum, you will be able to see light. This will help a cultivator progress toward high levels. Those who can't see clearly will be able to remedy this through cultivation.

People who have less quintessential *qi* only see images in black and white through the Third Eye. The Third Eye of a person who has relatively more quintessential *qi* will be able to see scenes in color and in clearer form. The more the quintessential *qi*, the better the clarity. But every individual is different. Some people are born with the Third Eye open, while for others it might be tightly clogged. When the Third Eye is opening, the image is similar to the blooming of a flower, opening layer after layer. You will initially discover during the seated meditation that there is illumination in the area of the Third Eye. At the beginning the illumination isn't so bright, while later it turns red. The Third Eye of some people is tightly closed, so their initial physical

15

reactions might be quite strong. These people will feel the muscles around the primary passage and the Shangen point tightening, as if they were being pressed and squeezed inward. Their temples and foreheads will start to feel like they are swelling and aching. All of these are symptoms of the Third Eye opening. A person whose Third Eye opens easily can occasionally see certain things. During my classes, some people unwittingly see my Law Bodies. They disappear when they intentionally try to look, as these people are then actually using their physical eyes. When you see some things with your eyes closed, try to remain in that state of seeing and you will gradually see things more clearly. If you want to watch more closely, you will actually switch to your own eyes and use the optic nerves. You will then be unable to see anything.

The dimensions perceived by the Third Eye differ in accordance with the level of a person's Third Eye. Some scientific research departments fail to understand this principle, preventing some *qigong* experiments from reaching their expected outcomes. Occasionally, some experiments even reach opposite conclusions. For example, an institute designed a method to test supernormal abilities. They asked *qigong* masters to see the contents of a sealed box. Because those masters' Third Eye levels are different, their answers are different. The research staff then regarded the Third Eye as false and as a misleading concept. Someone with a lower-level Third Eye will usually achieve better results in this kind of experiment, because his Third Eye is opened at the level of the Celestial Eyesight—a level suitable only for observing objects in this physical dimension. So people who don't understand the Third Eye think that these people have the greatest supernormal abilities. All objects, organic or inorganic, appear in different shapes and forms in different dimensions. For example, as soon as a glass is manufactured, in a different dimension an intelligent entity comes into existence. Moreover, prior to existing as this entity it might have been something else. When the Third Eye is at its lowest level, one will see the glass. At a high level one will see the entity that exists in the other dimension. At an even higher level one will see the material form prior to the existence of that intelligent entity.

(3) Remote Viewing

After opening the Third Eye, the supernormal ability of Remote Viewing emerges for some people, and they are able to see objects thousands of miles away. Each individual occupies dimensions of his own. In those dimensions he is as big as a universe. Within a certain particular dimension, he has a mirror in front of his forehead, though it is invisible in our dimension. Everyone has this mirror, but the mirror of a nonpractitioner faces inward. For practitioners, this mirror slowly turns over. Once it turns over, the mirror can reflect what the practitioner wants to see. In his particular dimension he is rather large. Since his body is fairly large, so too is his mirror. Whatever the cultivator wants to see can be reflected onto the mirror. Although the image has been captured, he still can't see, as the image needs to stay on the mirror for a second. The mirror turns over and allows him to see the objects it reflects. Then it turns back, flipping back over quickly, and flipping back and forth ceaselessly. Cinematic film moves at twenty-four frames per second to produce continuous movement. The speed at which the mirror flips is much faster than that, and so the images appear continuous and clear. This is Remote Viewing—the principle of Remote Viewing is this simple. This used to be very secret, yet I have revealed it in just a few lines.

(4) Dimensions

From our perspective, dimensions are quite complicated. Humankind knows only the dimension in which humans currently exist, while other dimensions haven't yet been explored or detected. When it comes to other dimensions, we *qigong* masters have already seen dozens of levels of dimensions. These, too, can be explained theoretically, though they remain unproven by science. Even though some people don't admit the existence of certain things, they have actually reflected into our dimension. For example, there is a place called the Bermuda Triangle (the Devil's Triangle). Some ships and planes have disappeared in that area, only to reemerge years later. No one can explain why, as no one has gone beyond the confines of human thoughts and theories. In fact, the Triangle is a gateway to another dimension. Unlike our regular doors that have definite positions, it remains in an unpredictable state. The ship can easily enter the other dimension if it passes through when the door happens to be open. Humans cannot sense the differences between the dimensions, and they enter into the other dimension instantly. The space-time difference between that dimension and our dimension cannot be expressed in miles—a distance of thousands of miles might be contained in one point here, that is, they might exist in the same place and at the same time. The ship swings in for a moment and comes back out again by accident. Yet decades have passed in this world, since time is different in these two dimensions. There are also unitary worlds existing in each dimension. There is a similarity here to our models of atomic structures wherein one ball is connected to another by a string, involving many balls and strings; it is very complex.

A British pilot was carrying out a mission four years prior to World War II. In the middle of his flight he ran into a heavy thunderstorm. By drawing on past experience, he was able to find an abandoned airport. The moment the airport appeared before his eyes, a completely different picture came into view: All of a sudden it was sunny and cloudless, as if he had just emerged from another world. The airplanes at the airport were colored in yellow, and people were busy doing things on the ground. He thought this was so weird! No one acknowledged him after he touched down; even the control tower didn't contact him. The pilot then decided to leave since the sky had cleared up. He flew again, and when he was at the same distance at which he had seen the airport moments ago, he again plunged into a thunderstorm. He eventually managed to get back. He reported the situation and even wrote it down in the flight record. But his superiors didn't believe him. Four years later World War II broke out, and he was transferred to that abandoned airport. He immediately recalled that it was exactly the same scene he had seen four years before. All of us *qigong* masters know how to explain it. He did in advance what he would do four years later. Before the first action had begun, he had gone there and played his role in advance. Things then returned to being in the right order.

5. Qigong Treatments and Hospital Treatments

Theoretically speaking, *qigong* treatments are completely different from the treatments given at hospitals. Western treatments utilize methods of everyday people's society. Despite having means such as laboratory tests and X-ray examinations, they can only observe the sources of illness in this dimension and they cannot see fundamental causes that exist in other dimensions. So they fail to understand the cause of illness. Medication can remove or drive away the origin of a patient's illness (which is considered a pathogen by Western doctors, and karma in *qigong*) if he or she isn't seriously ill. Medicine will be ineffective in the event that the illness is

---

[19] Li Shizhen (lee shr-juhn), Sun Simiao (sun szz-meow), Bian Que (byen chueh), and Huatuo (hwa-toah)—famous doctors of Chinese medicine in ancient times.

19

serious, as the patient might be unable to bear increased dosages. Not all illnesses are constrained by the laws of this world. Some illnesses are quite serious and exceed the confines of this world, rendering hospitals incapable of curing them.

Chinese Medicine is the traditional medical science in our country. It is inseparable from the supernormal abilities developed through cultivation of the human body. Ancient people paid special attention to cultivation of the human body. The Confucian School, the Dao School, the Buddha School—and even the students of Confucianism—have all attached importance to meditation. Sitting in meditation used to be considered a skill. Even though they didn't perform exercises, over the course of time they still developed their *gong* and supernormal abilities. Why was Chinese acupuncture able to detect the human body's meridians so clearly? Why aren't the acupuncture points connected horizontally? Why aren't they crossed, and why are they connected vertically? Why were they able to be mapped out with such accuracy? Modern people with supernormal abilities can see with their own eyes the same things that those Chinese doctors portrayed. This is because the famous ancient Chinese doctors generally had supernormal abilities. In Chinese history, Li Shizhen, Sun Simiao, Bian Que, and Hua Tuo[19] were all in fact *qigong* masters with supernormal abilities. In being passed down to this day, Chinese Medicine has lost its supernormal ability component and has only retained the treatment techniques. In the past, Chinese doctors used their eyes (with supernormal abilities) to diagnose illness. Later, they also developed the method of taking pulses.[20] If supernormal abilities were added back into the Chinese methods of treatment, one could say that Western Medicine wouldn't be able to catch up with

---

[20] In Chinese Medicine, pulse diagnosis is a complicated art used to evaluate the vitality of each individual internal organ of the body.

20

Chinese Medicine for many years to come.

Qigong treatments eliminate the root cause of illness. I regard illness as one type of karma, and to treat an illness is to help diminish this karma. Some *qigong* masters treat illness by using the method of discharging and supplementing *qi* to help patients eliminate black *qi*. At a rather low level these masters discharge black *qi*, yet they don't know the root cause of the black *qi*. This black *qi* will return and the illness will relapse. The truth is that the black *qi* is not the cause of the illness—the existence of black *qi* only makes the patient feel uncomfortable. The root cause of the patient's illness is an intelligent entity that exists in another dimension. Many *qigong* masters don't know this. Since that intelligent entity is mighty, average people are not able touch it, nor would they dare to. Falun Gong's way of treatment focuses on and starts with that intelligent entity, removing the root cause of the illness. Moreover, a shield is installed in that area so that the illness will be unable to invade again.

Qigong can heal illness but it can't interfere with the conditions of human society. It would interfere with the conditions of everyday people's society if it were applied on a large scale, and that is not allowed; its healing effects wouldn't be good either. As you may know, some people have opened *qigong* diagnostic clinics, *qigong* hospitals, and *qigong* rehabilitation centers. Their treatments might have been quite effective before they opened these businesses. Once they open a business to treat illnesses, the effectiveness plummets. This means that people are prohibited from using supernatural methods to fulfill the functions of everyday people's society. Doing so certainly reduces their effectiveness to a level as low as the methods of everyday people's society.

---

[21] Cao Cao (tsaow-tsaow)—an emperor during the Three Kingdoms period (220 - 265 A.D.).

A person can use supernormal abilities to observe the inside of a human body layer by layer, similar to how medical cross sectioning is done. Soft tissues and any other part of the body can be seen. Though the current CAT scan is able to see clearly, the use of a machine is still required; it is really time consuming, uses a great deal of film, and is quite slow and costly. It is not as convenient or accurate as human supernormal abilities. By closing their eyes to do a quick scan, *qigong* masters are able to see any part of the patient directly and clearly. Isn't this high tech? This is even more advanced than what is considered high tech today. Yet this kind of skill already existed in ancient China—it was the "high tech" of ancient times. Hua Tuo discovered a tumor on Cao Cao's[21] brain and wanted to perform surgery on him. Cao Cao had Hua Tuo arrested, because he couldn't believe it and mistook it as a way to harm him. Cao Cao eventually died as a result of the brain tumor. Many great Chinese doctors in history really possessed supernormal abilities. It is just that people in this modern society zealously pursue practical things and have forgotten the ancient traditions.

Our high-level *qigong* cultivation should reexamine traditional things, inherit and develop them through our practice, and reuse them to benefit human society.

6. Buddha School Qigong and Buddhism

Many people think of a matter as soon as we mention Buddha School *qigong*: Since the goal of the Buddha School is to cultivate

---

[22] Fo Tuo (foah-toah)—"Buddha."

[23] *Ci Hai* (tsz high)—the name of an authoritative Chinese dictionary.

Buddhahood, they start to relate it to the things of Buddhism. I hereby solemnly clarify that Falun Gong is *qigong* of the Buddha School. It is a righteous, great cultivation way and has nothing to do with Buddhism. Buddha School *qigong* is Buddha School *qigong*, while Buddhism is Buddhism. They take different paths, even though they have the same goal in cultivation. They are different schools of practice with different requirements. I mentioned the word "Buddha," and I will mention it again later when I teach the practice at higher levels. The word itself doesn't have any superstitious overtones. Some people can't tolerate hearing the word Buddha, and claim that we propagate superstition. It is not so. "Buddha" began as a Sanskrit term that originated in India. It was translated into Chinese according to its pronunciation and called Fo Tuo.[22] People omitted the word "Tuo" and kept the "Fo." Translated into Chinese it means "Enlightened One"—a person who is enlightened. (Refer to the *Ci Hai*[23] dictionary.)

(1) Buddha School Qigong

At present, two types of Buddha School *qigong* have been made public. One separated from Buddhism and has produced many distinguished monks throughout its thousands of years of development. When its practitioners have cultivated to quite an advanced level, high-

---

[24] "Great Cultural Revolution"—a communist political movement in China that denounced traditional values and culture (1966-1976).

[25] Sakyamuni—Buddha Sakyamuni, or "the Buddha," Siddhartha Gautama. Popularly known as the founder of Buddhism, he lived in ancient India around the 5th century B.C.

[26] *samadhi*—Buddhist meditation.

level masters will come to teach them something so that they will receive genuine instruction from even higher levels. All of the things in Buddhism used to be passed down to one individual at a time. Only when he was near the end of his life would a distinguished monk pass these down to one disciple, who would cultivate according to Buddhist doctrines, improving holistically. This type of *qigong* seemed closely connected to Buddhism. Monks were driven out of the temples later, namely, during the time of the Great Cultural Revolution.[24] These exercises then spread to the general public where they developed in number.

Another type of *qigong* is also of the Buddha School. Over the ages, this type has never been a part of Buddhism. It has always been practiced quietly, either among the populace or deep in the mountains. These kinds of practices have their uniqueness. They need to choose a good disciple—someone with tremendous virtue who is truly capable of cultivating to an advanced level. This kind of person appears in this world only once in many, many years. These practices cannot be made public, as they require rather high *xinxing* and their *gong* develops rapidly. These sorts of practices are not few. The same applies to the Dao School. Daoist *qigong*, while all belonging to the Dao School, are further divided into Kunlung, Emei, Wudang, etc. There are different

---

[27] Dharma—this is a conventional translation for the Chinese word "Fa," as used in the context of Buddhism.

[28] Mahayana—"The Great Vehicle Buddhism."

[29] Tathagata—enlightened being with Attainment Status in the Buddha School who is above the levels of Bodhisattva and Arhat.

[30] Bodhisattva—enlightened being with Attainment Status in the Buddha School who is higher than Arhat but lower than Tathagata.

subdivisions within each group, and the subdivisions are quite different from one another. They cannot be mixed and practiced together.

(2) Buddhism

Buddhism is a system of cultivation practice that Sakyamuni[25] enlightened to on his own in India more than two thousand years ago, and it is based on his original cultivation practice. It can be summarized in three words: precept, *samadhi*,[26] wisdom. Precepts are for the purpose of *samadhi*. Buddhism does in fact have exercises though it doesn't discuss the matter. Buddhists are indeed performing exercises when they sit in meditation and enter a state of tranquility. This is because energy from the universe will start to gather around a person's body when he calms down and settles his mind, and this achieves the effect of performing *qigong* exercises. The precepts in Buddhism are for abandoning all human desires and discarding everything to which an everyday person is attached so that the monk can reach a state of peacefulness and stillness, enabling him to enter *samadhi*. A person continuously improves himself in *samadhi*, until he eventually becomes enlightened, with his wisdom emerging. He will then know the universe and see its truth.

---

[31] Han (hahn) area—Han people comprise the largest ethnic group in China, and the "Han area" is used to refer to the area that they occupy; that is, most central provinces and regions of China (i.e., Tibet, etc.).

[32] Xinjiang (shin-jyang)—a province in northwestern China.

[33] Huichang (hway-chahng)—Emperor Wu Zong's time of rule during the Tang Dynasty (841 - 846 A.D.).

Sakyamuni did only three things daily when he was teaching: he taught Dharma[27] (primarily the Dharma of Arhat) to his disciples, carried a bowl to collect alms (beg for food), and cultivated through sitting in meditation. After Sakyamuni left this world, Brahmanism and Buddhism battled. These two religions later merged into one, called Hinduism. Buddhism no longer exists in India today as a result of this. Mahayana[28] Buddhism appeared through later developments and changes and was spread to inner China, where it has become today's Buddhism. Mahayana Buddhism doesn't worship Sakyamuni as its sole founder—it is a multi-Buddha faith. It believes in many Tathagatas,[29] such as Buddha Amitabha, Medicine Buddha, etc., and there are more precepts now, while the goal of cultivation has become higher. Back in his time, Sakyamuni taught the Dharma of Bodhisattva[30] to a few disciples. These teachings were later reorganized and have developed into today's Mahayana Buddhism, which is for cultivating to the realm of Bodhisattva. The tradition of Theravada Buddhism has been retained to this day in Southeast Asia, and ceremonies are performed using supernormal abilities. In Buddhism's course of evolution, one cultivation way branched off to the Tibet region of our country and is called Tibetan Tantrism. Another cultivation way spread to the Han area[31] via Xinjiang[32] and was called Tang Tantrism (this disappeared after Buddhism was suppressed during the years of Huichang[33]). Another branch in India evolved into yoga.

No exercises are taught in Buddhism and *qigong* is not practiced. This is to preserve the traditional method of Buddhist cultivation. It is also an important reason why Buddhism has lasted more than two thousand years without waning. It has naturally maintained its own tradition precisely because it hasn't accepted into it anything foreign. In Buddhism there are different ways to cultivate. Theravada Buddhism focuses on self-salvation and self-cultivation; Mahayana Buddhism has evolved to offer salvation to both self and others—salvation of all sentient beings.

7. Righteous Cultivation Ways and Evil Ways

(1) The Side-Door Awkward Ways (*Pangmen Zuodao*)

The Side-Door Awkward Ways are also called the Unconventional (*Qimen*) Cultivation Ways. Various *qigong* cultivation ways existed prior to the establishment of religions. There are many practices outside of religions that have spread among the populace. Most of them lack systematic doctrines and so have not become complete cultivation systems. Nonetheless, the Unconventional Cultivation Ways have their own systematic, complete, and unusually intense cultivation methods, and they, too, have been spread among the populace. These practice systems are usually called the Side-Door Awkward Ways. Why are they called this? Pangmen literally means "side door"; and Zuodao means "awkward ways." People consider both the Buddha and Dao School cultivation ways to be straight ways, with all others being side-door awkward ways or wicked cultivation ways. Actually, it isn't so. The Side-Door Awkward Ways have been practiced secretly throughout history, being taught to one disciple at a time. They weren't allowed to be revealed to the public. Once made known, people would not understand them very well. Even their practitioners hold that they are of neither the Buddha nor the Dao School. The cultivation principles of the unconventional ways have strict *xinxing* criteria. They cultivate according to the nature of the universe, advocating doing kind deeds and watching one's *xinxing*. The highly accomplished masters in these practices all have unique skills, and some of their unique techniques are powerful. I have met three highly accomplished masters from the Unconventional Cultivation Ways who taught me some things that

27

cannot be found in either the Buddha or Dao School. These things were each fairly difficult to practice during the process of cultivation, so the *gong* obtained was unique. In contrast, strict *xinxing* criteria are lacking among some so-called Buddha and Dao School cultivation methods, and as a result their practitioners cannot cultivate to an advanced level. So we should look at each cultivation method objectively.

(2) Martial Arts Qigong

Martial arts *qigong* is born of a long history. Having its own complete system of theories and cultivation methods, it has formed an independent system. Yet strictly speaking, it only manifests supernormal abilities that are generated by internal cultivation at the lowest level. All of the supernormal abilities that appear in martial arts cultivation also appear in internal cultivation. Martial arts cultivation also begins with doing *qi* exercises. For instance, when striking a piece of rock, in the beginning the martial arts practitioner needs to swing his arms to move *qi*. Over time, his *qi* will change in nature and become an energy mass that appears to exist in the form of light. At this point his *gong* will start to function. *Gong* has intelligence because it is an evolved matter. It exists in another dimension and is controlled by the thoughts coming from one's brain. When attacked, the martial arts practitioner doesn't need to move *qi*; *gong* will come merely with a thought. Over the course of cultivation his *gong* will continually be strengthened, with its particles becoming finer and its energy growing greater. The skills of Iron Sand Palm and Cinnabar Palm will appear. As we can see from movies, magazines, and television shows, the skills of Golden Bell Shield and Iron Cloth Shirt have emerged in recent years. These stem from the simultaneous practice of internal cultivation and martial

---

[34] *dantian* (dahn-t'yen)—"field of *dan*," located at the lower abdominal area.

arts cultivation. They come from cultivating internally and externally at the same time. To cultivate internally, a person needs to value virtue and cultivate his or her *xinxing*. Explained from a theoretical angle, when a person's ability reaches a certain level, *gong* will emit from the body's interior to its exterior. It will become a protective shield because of its high density. In terms of principles, the biggest difference between the martial arts and our internal cultivation lies in the fact that the martial arts are performed with vigorous movements and practitioners do not enter into tranquility. Not being tranquil makes *qi* flow underneath the skin and pass through the muscles instead of flowing into a person's *dantian*.[34] So they don't cultivate life, and neither are they able to.

(3) Reverse Cultivation and Gong Borrowing

Some people have never practiced *qigong*. Then suddenly they acquire *gong* overnight and have quite strong energy, and they can even heal illnesses for others. People call them *qigong* masters and they, too, go about teaching others. Some of them, despite the fact that they have never learned *qigong* or have only learned a few of its movements, are teaching people things that they have modified slightly. This kind of person is not qualified to be a *qigong* master. He or she doesn't have anything to pass on to others. What he or she teaches certainly can't be used to cultivate to a high level; the most it can do is help get rid of sickness and improve health. How does this kind of *gong* come about? Let's first talk about reverse cultivation. The commonly known phrase "reverse cultivation" pertains to those good people who have extremely high *xinxing*. They are usually older, such as over fifty years of age. There isn't enough time for them to cultivate from the beginning, as it is not easy to meet excellent masters who teach *qigong* exercises that cultivate both mind and body. The moment this type of person wants to cultivate, high-level masters will place a great amount of *gong* onto this person according to his or her *xinxing* foundation. This enables cultivation in reverse, from the top down, and this way it is much faster. From another dimension, high-level masters perform the transformation and continuously add *gong* to the person from the outside of his or her body; this is particularly the case when the person is giving treatments and forming an energy field. The *gong* given by the masters flows as if through a pipeline. Some people don't even know where the *gong* comes from. This is reverse cultivation.

Another type is called "*gong* borrowing," and this isn't restricted in terms of age. A human being has an Assistant Consciousness (*fu yishi*) along with a Main Consciousness (*zhu yishi*), and it is generally at a higher level than the Main Consciousness. The Assistant Consciousnesses of some people have reached such high levels that they can communicate with enlightened beings. When these kinds of people want to cultivate, their Assistant Consciousnesses also want to improve their levels and will immediately get in touch with those enlightened beings to borrow *gong* from them. After the *gong* is loaned this person will get it overnight. After obtaining the *gong*, he or she will be able to treat people to ease their pains. The person will usually employ the method of forming an energy field. He or she will also be able to give energy to people individually and to teach some techniques.

People like this usually start out being pretty good. Because they possess *gong*, they become well known and acquire both fame and personal gain. Attachments to renown and to personal gain come to occupy a substantial portion of their thinking—more than cultivation does. From that point on their *gong* starts to diminish, becoming smaller and smaller until finally it is all gone.

(4) Cosmic Language

Some people are suddenly able to speak a certain type of language. It sounds fairly fluent when it is uttered, yet it's not the language of any human society. What's it called? It is referred to as celestial language. This thing called "cosmic language" is in fact merely the language of those entities that are not so high. This phenomenon is occurring right now for quite a few *qigong* practitioners around the country; some of them can even speak several different languages. Of course, the languages of our humankind are also sophisticated and there are more than a thousand varieties. Is cosmic language considered a supernormal ability? I would say that it doesn't count as one. It isn't a supernormal ability that comes from you, and neither is it a kind of ability that's given to you from the outside. Rather, it is manipulation by foreign entities. These entities originate at a somewhat higher level—at least higher than that of humankind. It is one of them who does the talking, as the person who speaks cosmic language only serves as a medium. Most people do not even know themselves what they are saying. Only those who have mind-reading abilities can get a general sense of what the words mean. It is not a supernormal ability, but many people who have spoken these languages feel superior and elated since they think it is a supernormal ability. In fact, someone with a high-level Third Eye can definitely observe that a living entity is speaking from diagonally above, through the person's mouth.

That entity teaches the person to speak a cosmic language while passing on to him or her some of its energy. Yet thereafter this person will be under its control, so this is not a righteous cultivation way. Even though that entity is in a slightly higher dimension, it is not cultivating a righteous way. It therefore doesn't know how to teach cultivators to stay healthy or heal illnesses. Consequently, it utilizes this method of sending out energy through speech. Because it is dispersed, this energy has little power. It is effective in treating minor sicknesses but fails with serious diseases. Buddhism speaks of how those above cannot cultivate since they lack suffering and discord; moreover, they cannot temper themselves and are unable to improve their levels. So they look for ways to help people gain better health and thereby elevate themselves. This is what speaking cosmic language is all about. It is neither a supernormal ability nor *qigong*.

(5) Spirit Possession

The most injurious type of spirit possession (*futi*) is that by a low-level entity. This is caused by cultivating an evil way. It is really harmful to people, and the consequences of people being possessed are frightening. Not long after beginning to practice, some people become obsessed with treating patients and becoming rich; they think of these things all the time. These people might have originally been pretty decent or already had a master looking after them. Nevertheless, things turn sour when they start to contemplate giving treatments and getting rich. They then attract this type of entity. Even though it's not in our physical dimension it really exists.

This kind of practitioner suddenly feels that the Third Eye has opened and that he or she now has *gong*, but it is actually that the possessing spirit has control of his or her brain. It reflects onto this person's brain the images that it sees, making him or her feel that the Third Eye has opened. The person's Third Eye has not in fact opened whatsoever. Why does the possessing spirit or animal want to give this person *gong*? Why does it want to help him or her? It's because in our universe animals are forbidden to cultivate. Animals are not allowed to obtain a righteous cultivation way since they know nothing about *xinxing* and can't improve themselves. As a result, they want to attach themselves to human bodies and acquire the human essence. There is also another rule in this universe, namely: no loss, no gain. So they want to satisfy your desire for fame and personal gain. They will make you rich and famous, but they will not help you for nothing. They also want to gain something: your essence. You will have nothing left by the time they leave you and you will have turned very weak or become a vegetable. This is caused by your degenerate *xinxing*. One right mind will subdue a hundred evils. When you are righteous you will not attract evil. In other words, be a noble practitioner, turn away from all nonsense, and practice only a righteous cultivation way.

(6) A Righteous Practice Can Become a Wicked Cultivation Way

Although the practice systems some people learn come from righteous cultivation ways, people can actually practice wicked ways inadvertently due to their inability to impose strict self-requirements, to their failure to cultivate *xinxing*, and to their entertaining negative thoughts while performing their exercises. For example, when a person is performing the exercises there in either the standing stance or the seated meditation, his thoughts are actually on money, becoming well known, personal gain, or "he's wronged me, and I'll fix him after I acquire supernormal abilities." Or he is thinking of this or that supernormal ability, adding something very bad to his practice and actually practicing a wicked way. This is quite dangerous since it might attract some rather negative things, like low-level entities. Perhaps the person doesn't even know he has invited them. His attachment is strong; it is unacceptable to purposefully practice cultivation to fulfill one's desires. He isn't righteous, and even his master will be

---

[35] Falun Xiulian Dafa (fah-lun shyo-lien dah-fah)—"The Law Wheel Great Way of Cultivation Practice."

unable to protect him. So practitioners must maintain their *xinxing* strictly, keeping a righteous mind and craving nothing. Doing otherwise might incur problems.

Chapter II
Falun Gong

Falun Gong originates from Falun Xiulian Dafa[35] in the Buddha School. It is one of the Buddha School's special *qigong* methods, yet it has its own distinctive qualities that set it apart from the average ways of cultivation in the Buddha School. This cultivation system is a special, intense cultivation method that used to require that cultivators have extremely high *xinxing* and great inborn quality. In order for more practitioners to improve while also meeting the needs of a massive number of dedicated cultivators, I have redesigned and made public this set of cultivation methods that are now suitable for popularization. Despite the modifications, this practice still far exceeds other practices, their teachings, and levels.

1. The Falun's Function

The Falun of Falun Gong has the same nature as the universe, for it is a miniature of the universe. Cultivators of Falun Gong not only rapidly develop their supernormal abilities and *gong* potency, they also develop an incomparably powerful Falun in a brief period of time. Once developed, one's Falun exists as an intelligent entity. It automatically spins ceaselessly in the practitioner's lower abdominal area, constantly absorbing and transforming energy from the universe and ultimately converting the energy in the practitioner's original-body into *gong*. Consequently, the effect of "the Fa refines the practitioner" is achieved. This means that the Falun constantly refines this person even though he or she doesn't perform the exercises every minute. Internally, the Falun offers salvation to oneself. It makes a person stronger and healthier, more intelligent and wise, and it protects the practitioner from deviation. It can also protect the cultivator from interference by people with inferior *xinxing*. Externally, the Falun can both heal sicknesses and eliminate evils for others, rectifying all abnormal conditions. The Falun rotates continuously in the lower abdominal area, turning clockwise nine times and then counterclockwise nine times. When rotating clockwise, it vigorously absorbs energy from the universe and that energy is very strong. Its rotational power becomes stronger as a person's *gong* potency improves. This is a state that can't be attained by deliberate attempts to pour *qi* into the top of the head. When rotating counterclockwise, it releases energy and provides salvation to all beings, rectifying abnormal states. People around the practitioner benefit. Of all the *qigong* practices taught in our country, Falun Gong is the first and only cultivation method that has achieved "the Fa refines the practitioner."

The Falun is most precious and could not be exchanged for

any amount of money. When my master passed the Falun on to me, he told me that the Falun shouldn't be passed on to anyone else; even those people who have cultivated for a thousand years or more want to have it, but cannot. This cultivation system can only be passed on to one person after a very, very long time, unlike those that are passed on to one person every few decades. The Falun is therefore extremely precious. It is still extremely precious even though we have now made it public and altered it to become less powerful. Cultivators who have acquired it are halfway through their cultivation. The only thing that remains is for you to improve your *xinxing*, and quite an advanced level awaits you. Of course, people who are not predestined might stop after cultivating for a little while, and then the Falun in them will cease to exist.

Falun Gong is of the Buddha School, but it far exceeds the scope of the Buddha School: Falun Gong cultivates according to the entire universe. In the past, cultivation in the Buddha School only mentioned principles of the Buddha School, while cultivation in the Dao School only addressed principles of the Dao School. Neither thoroughly explained the universe at its fundamental level. The universe is similar to human beings in that it has its own nature, along with its material composition. This nature can be summarized in three words: Zhen-Shan-Ren. Dao School cultivation focuses its understanding on Zhen: telling the truth, doing honest deeds, returning to the origin and one's true self, and finally becoming a true person. Buddha School cultivation focuses on Shan: developing great compassion, and offering salvation to all beings. Our cultivation way cultivates Zhen, Shan, and Ren simultaneously, directly cultivating according to the

---

[36] Taiji (tye-jee)—the symbol of the Dao School, popularly referred to in the West as the "yin-yang" symbol.

fundamental nature of the universe and eventually assimilating practitioners to the universe.

Falun Gong is a cultivation system of both mind and body; when a practitioner's *gong* potency and *xinxing* have reached a certain level, he or she is bound to attain in this world both Enlightenment (the state of Unlocking Gong (*kaigong*)) and an indestructible body. In general, Falun Gong is divided into In-Triple-World-Law and Beyond-Triple-World-Law, which include many levels. I hope that all devoted practitioners will cultivate diligently and continually improve their *xinxing* so that they can reach Consummation.

2. The Falun's Configuration

The Falun of Falun Gong is an intelligent, spinning body of high-energy substances. It rotates according to the order of the entire grand movements of the cosmos. In a sense, the Falun is a miniature of the universe.

In the center of the Falun there is a Buddha School symbol of *srivatsa*, 卍, (in Sanskrit, *srivatsa* means "the gathering of all good fortune" (refer to the *Ci Hai* dictionary)), which is the core of the Falun. Its color is close to golden yellow, and its base color is bright red. The base color of the outer ring is orange. Four Taiji[36] symbols and four Buddha School *srivatsa* are arranged alternately in eight directions. The Taiji that consist of red and black colors belong to the Dao School, while the Taiji consisting

---

[37] *Dan* (dahn)—an energy cluster which forms in the bodies of some cultivators in internal alchemy; in external alchemy, it is referred to as the "Elixir of Immortality."

of red and blue are of the Great Primordial Dao School. The four small *srivatsa* are also golden yellow. The base color of the Falun changes periodically from red, to orange, to yellow, green, blue, indigo, and violet. These are extraordinarily beautiful colors (refer to the color insert). The colors of the central *srivatsa*, 卍, and the Taiji do not change. These *srivatsa*, 卍, of different sizes rotate on their own, as does the Falun. The Falun is rooted in the universe. The universe is rotating, all galaxies are rotating, and so the Falun is also rotating. Those whose Third Eye are at lower levels can see the Falun spinning like a fan; those whose Third Eye are at higher levels can see the whole image of the Falun, which is extraordinarily beautiful and brilliant, and this encourages practitioners to cultivate more diligently and make faster progress.

3. Characteristics of Falun Gong Cultivation

(1) The Fa Refines the Practitioner

People who practice Falun Gong are able to not only rapidly develop their *gong* potency and supernormal abilities, but also to procure a Falun through cultivation. The Falun can form in a short period of time, and once formed it is quite powerful. It can protect practitioners from going awry as well as from interference by people with inferior *xinxing*. The principles of Falun Gong are completely different from those of conventional cultivation

---

[38] *Qigong* systems that cultivate *dan*.

[39] *sarira*—the special remains that are left behind after certain cultivators are cremated.

[40] Niwan (nee-wahn) Palace—a Daoist term for the pineal gland.

methods. This is because after a Falun forms, it rotates ceaselessly on its own; it exists in the form of an intelligent entity, continuously collecting energy in the practitioner's lower abdominal area. The Falun automatically absorbs energy from the universe by rotating. The Falun achieves the goal of "the Fa refines the practitioner" precisely because it rotates incessantly, which means that the Falun cultivates people ceaselessly even though they don't perform the exercises every moment. As you all know, everyday people have to work during the day and rest at night. This leaves limited time for exercises. Thinking about performing exercises all the time certainly won't serve the purpose of continuous performance twenty-four hours a day. The goal of around-the-clock performance cannot be fulfilled by any other method. Yet the Falun rotates ceaselessly, and when rotating inward it absorbs a great amount of *qi* (energy's initial form of existence). Day and night, the Falun keeps storing and transforming the absorbed *qi* in each and every location of the Falun. It converts *qi* into high-level substances, ultimately changing it in the cultivator's body into *gong*. This is "the Fa refines the practitioner." Falun Gong's cultivation is entirely different from all other practice systems or *qigong* cultivation methods, which cultivate *dan*.[37]

The principal feature of Falun Gong is its cultivation of a Falun rather than *dan*. Until now, all the cultivation methods that have been made public, regardless of which school or cultivation way they have come from—be they branches of Buddhism or Daoism, of the Buddha or Dao School, or of the ways spread among people— cultivate *dan*. So do many side-door cultivation ways. They are called *dan*-method *qigong*.[38] The cultivation used by monks, nuns, and Daoists has taken this path of cultivating *dan*. If these persons are cremated at death, they produce *sarira*,[39] which are composed of a hard and beautiful substance that modern scientific equipment cannot discern. Actually, they are a high-energy substance, gathered from other dimensions—not our dimension. That is *dan*.

39

It is very difficult for those who practice *dan*-method *qigong* to achieve Enlightenment during the person's lifetime. It used to be that many people who practiced *dan*-method *qigong* tried to lift their *dan*. It couldn't be lifted out once it was raised to the Niwan Palace,[40] and so these people got stuck here. Some people wanted to deliberately burst it but they had no way of doing so. There were some cases like this: A person's grandfather didn't succeed in cultivation, so at the end of his lifetime he spat the *dan* out and passed it on to this person's father; his father didn't succeed in cultivation, so at the end of his lifetime he spat it out and passed it on to this person. To this day the person still hasn't achieved much. It's really difficult! Of course, there are many decent cultivation methods. It's not so bad if you can receive genuine teaching from someone, but chances are he or she won't teach you high-level things.

(2) Cultivating the Main Consciousness

Everyone has a Main Consciousness. One usually relies on one's Main Consciousness in order to act and think. In addition to the Main Consciousness, one also has one or more Assistant Consciousnesses and inherited spirits from one's ancestors. The Assistant Consciousness(es) has the same name as the Main Consciousness, but in general it is more capable and of a higher level. It doesn't become deluded by our human society and it can see its own particular dimension. Many cultivation methods take the route of cultivating the Assistant Consciousness, whereby one's flesh body and Main Consciousness only function as a vehicle. These practitioners generally don't know about these things, and they even feel good about themselves. It is incredibly difficult for one to break with practical things while living in society, particularly the things that a person is attached to. Therefore, many cultivation methods emphasize performing exercises while in a state of trance—an absolute state of trance. When transformation occurs during a state of trance, the Assistant Consciousness in fact gets transformed in a different society and improved through this process. One day the Assistant Consciousness will complete its cultivation and take away your *gong*. Nothing is left for your Main Consciousness and your original-body, and your lifelong cultivation falls short of success. That's a great pity. Some well-known *qigong* masters command great supernormal abilities of all kinds, and along with these come prestige and respect. Yet they still don't know that their *gong* has not actually grown on their own bodies.

Our Falun Gong directly cultivates the Main Consciousness; we ensure that *gong* actually grows on your body. The Assistant Consciousness will of course also get a share; it also improves, while in the secondary position. Our cultivation method has strict *xinxing* criteria that allow you to temper your *xinxing* and improve while in human society, under the most complicated circumstances—like the lotus flower emerging out of mud. Because of this you can succeed in your cultivation. This is why Falun Gong is so precious: It is precious because it is you, yourself, who obtains *gong*. But it is also quite difficult. The difficulty lies in the fact that you have chosen a path which will temper and test you in the most complicated environment.

The Main Consciousness must always be used to direct one's cultivation, since the goal of our practice is to cultivate the Main Consciousness. The Main Consciousness should make decisions, rather than turning them over to the Assistant Consciousness. Otherwise, there would come a day when the Assistant Consciousness would complete its cultivation at a higher level and take your *gong*

41

with it, while your original-body and Main Consciousness would have nothing left. When you are cultivating to high levels, your Main Consciousness shouldn't become unaware of what you are doing, as if it were asleep. You need to be clear that you are the one performing the exercises, ascending through cultivation, and improving your *xinxing*—only then will you be in control and able to acquire *gong*. Sometimes when you are absentminded you might accomplish something without even knowing how it was done. It is actually your Assistant Consciousness that is taking effect; your Assistant Consciousness is in command. If you open your eyes to look about while you are sitting there in meditation and you see that there is another you across from you, then that is your Assistant Consciousness. If you are sitting there in meditation facing north, but all of a sudden you find that you are sitting on the north side, wondering, "How did I get out?", then this is your true self that has come out. What sits there is your flesh body and Assistant Consciousness. These can be distinguished.

You shouldn't become completely unaware of yourself when you perform the exercises of Falun Gong. Doing so is not in line with the great way of Falun Gong cultivation. You have to keep your mind clear when doing the exercises. Deviation won't occur during the practice if your Main Consciousness is strong, as nothing will really be able to harm you. Some things might come onto the body if the Main Consciousness is weak.

(3) Doing the Exercises Regardless of Direction and Time

Many cultivation methods are particular about at what time and toward which direction it's best to perform their exercises. We are not concerned with these things in the least. Falun Gong cultivation is done according to the nature of the universe and the

42

principles of the universe's evolution. So direction and time are not important. We are, in effect, situated in the Falun while doing the exercises, which is omni-directional and always rotating. Our Falun is synchronized with the universe. The universe is in motion, the Milky Way is in motion, the nine planets are revolving around the sun, and Earth itself is rotating. Which way is north, east, south or west? People living on the earth devised these directions. So you will be facing all directions no matter which direction you face.

Some people say that it's best to do the exercises at midnight, while some say that noon or another time is best. We aren't concerned with this, either, because the Falun cultivates you when you are not performing the exercises. The Falun is helping you cultivate at every moment—the Fa refines the practitioner. In *dan*-method *qigong*, people cultivate *dan*; in Falun Gong, it is the Fa that cultivates people. Do the exercises more when you have time, and do them less when you have less time. It is quite flexible.

4. Cultivation of Both Mind and Body

Falun Gong cultivates both the mind and the body. Performing the exercises changes a person's original-body first. The original-body will not be discarded. The Main Consciousness merges into one with the flesh body, achieving complete cultivation of one's entire being.

---

[41] Fujian Province—located in southeastern China.

43

(1) Changing One's Original-Body

A human body is composed of flesh, blood, and bones, with different molecular structures and components. The molecular composition of the human body is transformed into high-energy matter through cultivation. The human body is then no longer composed of its original substances, as it has undergone a change in its fundamental properties. But cultivators live and cultivate among everyday people and they can't disrupt the way human society is. So this kind of change alters neither the body's original molecular structure nor the sequence in which its molecules are arranged; it just changes the original molecular composition. The body's flesh remains soft, the bones are still hard, and the blood is still fluid. One will still bleed when cut with a knife. According to the Chinese Theory of the Five Elements, everything is composed of metal, wood, water, fire, and earth. The human body is no different. When a cultivator has undergone the changes in his or her original-body whereby high-energy substances replace the original molecular components, the human body at that point is no longer composed of its original substances. This is the principle behind what is known as "transcending the five elements."

The most noticeable feature of cultivation methods that cultivate both mind and body is that they prolong a person's life and deter aging. Our Falun Gong also has this noticeable feature. Falun

---

[42] Ren and Du—the Du channel, or "Governing Vessel," begins in the pelvic cavity and travels upward along the middle of the back. The Ren channel, or "Conception Vessel," travels upward from the pelvic cavity along the middle of the body's front side.

[43] eight Extra Meridians—in Chinese Medicine, these are meridians that exist in addition to the twelve Regular Meridians. Most of the eight Extra intersect with the acupuncture points of the twelve Regular, and so they are not considered independent or major meridians.

Gong works this way: It fundamentally changes the molecular composition of the human body, storing the gathered high-energy matter in each cell and ultimately allowing this high-energy matter to replace the cellular components. Metabolism will no longer occur. A person thus transcends the five elements, having turned his or her body into one composed of substances from other dimensions. This person will be young forever, as he or she is no longer restrained by our space-time.

There have been many accomplished monks in history who have had very long life spans. Now there are people who are hundreds of years old walking on the streets, only you can't tell who they are. You cannot distinguish them, as they look very young and wear the same clothes as everyday people. The human life span shouldn't be as short as it is now. Speaking from the perspective of modern science, people should be able to live for over two hundred years. According to records, there was a person in Britain named Femcath who lived for 207 years. A person in Japan named Mitsu Taira lived to be 242 years old. During the Tang Dynasty in our country, there was a monk called Hui Zhao who lived to be 290 years old. According to the county annals of Yong Tai in Fujian Province,[41] Chen Jun was born in the first year of Zhong He time (881 AD) under the reign of Emperor Xi Zong during the Tang Dynasty. He died in the Tai Ding time of the Yuan Dynasty (1324 AD), after living for 443 years. These

---

[44] Huiyin (hway-yin) point—the acupuncture point in the center of the perineum.

[45] Baihui (bye-hway) point—the acupuncture point located at the crown of one's head.

[46] *yin* (yin) and *yang* (yahng)—the Dao School believes that everything contains opposite forces of *yin* and *yang* which are mutually exclusive, yet interdependent, e.g., female (*yin*) vs. male (*yang*), front of the body (*yin*) vs. back of the body (*yang*).

are all backed up by records and can be investigated—they aren't fairy tales. Our Falun Gong practitioners have come to have noticeably fewer wrinkles on their faces, which now have a rosy, healthy glow, thanks to cultivation. Their bodies feel really light, and they are not a bit tired when walking or working. This is a common phenomenon. I myself have cultivated for decades and others say that my face hasn't changed much in twenty years. This is the reason. Our Falun Gong contains very powerful things for cultivating the body. Falun Gong cultivators look quite different in age from everyday people—they do not look their actual age. So the primary features of cultivation methods that cultivate both mind and body are: prolonging life, deterring aging, and lengthening people's life expectancy.

(2) The Falun Heavenly Circuit

Our human body is a small universe. The energy of the human body circles around the body, and this is called the circulation of the small universe, or the heavenly circulation. Speaking in terms of levels, connecting the two meridians of Ren and Du[42] is only a superficial heavenly circuit. It doesn't have the effect of cultivating the body. The Small Heavenly Circuit, in its true sense, circulates inside the body from the Niwan Palace to the *dantian*. Through this internal circulation, all of a person's meridians are opened up and expanded from the inside of the body to its outside. Our Falun Gong calls for all meridians to be open at the outset.

The Great Heavenly Circuit is the movement of the eight Extra Meridians,[43] and it goes around the entire body to complete one cycle. If the Great Heavenly Circuit is opened, it will bring about a state in which a person can levitate off the ground. This is what is meant by "ascending in broad daylight," as mentioned in *Scripture of Dan Cultivation*. Nevertheless, an area in your body

46

will usually be locked so that you will be unable to fly. Yet it will bring you to this state: You will walk quickly and effortlessly, and when you walk uphill you will feel as if someone were pushing you from behind. The opening of the Great Heavenly Circuit can also bring about a type of supernormal ability. It can enable the *qi* that exists in different organs of the body to exchange positions. The *qi* of the heart will move to the stomach, the *qi* of the stomach will travel to the intestines, and so on. As one's *gong* potency strengthens, if this ability is released outside the human body it will become the supernormal ability of telekinesis. This kind of heavenly circuit is also called the Meridian Heavenly Circuit, or the Heaven and Earth Heavenly Circuit. But its movement still won't achieve the goal of transforming the body. There has to be another corresponding heavenly circuit, called the Borderline Heavenly Circuit. Here is how the Borderline Heavenly Circuit moves: It emerges from either the Huiyin point[44] or the Baihui point[45] and travels along the sides of the body, where *yin* borders *yang*.[46]

The heavenly circuit in Falun Gong is much greater than the movement of the eight Extra Meridians that are discussed in regular cultivation methods. It is the movement of all the crisscrossing meridians located throughout the entire body. All meridians of the entire body need to be thoroughly opened at once, and they all have to move together. These things are already embedded in our Falun Gong, so you don't need to deliberately do them or guide them with your thoughts. You will go awry if you do it that way. During the lecture series, I install energy mechanisms outside your body that circulate automatically. The energy mechanisms are something unique to high-level cultivation, and they are part of what makes our exercises automatic. Just like the Falun, they revolve ceaselessly, leading all internal meridians into rotating motion. Even if you haven't worked on the heavenly circuit, those meridians have in fact already been driven into motion, and deep inside and outside they are all moving together. We use our exercises to strengthen the energy mechanisms that exist outside the body.

(3) Opening the Meridians

The objective of opening the meridians is to allow energy to circulate and to change the molecular composition of cells, transforming them into high-energy matter. The meridians of nonpractitioners are congested and narrow. The meridians of practitioners gradually brighten and have their congested areas cleared. The meridians of veteran practitioners widen, and they will widen even further during cultivation at higher levels. Some people have meridians as wide as a finger. Yet the opening up of meridians itself reflects neither one's cultivation level nor the height of one's *gong*. The meridians will be brightened and widened through performing the exercises, and eventually connect to become one large piece. At that point, this person will have no meridians or acupuncture points. Put another way, his or her entire body will be meridians and acupuncture points. Even this condition doesn't mean that this person has attained the Dao. It is only the manifestation of one level during the process of Falun Gong cultivation. Arrival at this stage signifies that this person has reached the end of In-Triple-World-Law cultivation. At the same time, this brings about a state quite noticeable from its outer appearance: Three Flowers Gathered Atop the Head (*sanhua juding*). The *gong* column will be rather high then and a great deal of supernormal abilities will have been developed, all of which possesses a shape and form. The three flowers appear on the crown of the head, with one resembling a chrysanthemum and another a lotus. The three flowers spin individually while

48

revolving around each other at the same time. Each flower has an extremely tall pole on top of it that reaches to the sky. These three poles also rotate and spin along with the flowers. The person will feel that his or her head has grown heavy. At this point the person will only have taken the last step of In-Triple-World-Law cultivation.

5. Mind-Intent

Falun Gong cultivation involves no use of mind-intent. A person's mind-intent doesn't accomplish anything by itself, though it can send out commands. What is really at work are supernormal abilities, which have the capacity of an intelligent being to think and can receive commands from the brain's signals. Yet many people, particularly those in *qigong* circles, have many different theories about it. They think that mind-intent can accomplish many things. Some talk about using mind-intent to develop supernormal abilities, using it to open the Third Eye, to heal illnesses, to perform telekinesis, etc. This is an incorrect understanding. At lower levels, everyday people use mind-intent to direct their sensory organs and four limbs. At higher levels, a cultivator's mind-intent elevates a notch and directs abilities around. In other words, supernormal abilities are dictated by mind-intent. This is how we look at mind-intent. Sometimes we see a *qigong* master giving treatments to others. Before the master moves a finger, the patients already acknowledge that they have become well, and they think that the healing is done through the master's mind-intent. In fact, that master releases a type of supernormal ability and dictates it to give the treatment or to do something else. Since supernormal abilities travel in another dimension, everyday people can't see them with their eyes. Those who don't know think that

49

it is mind-intent that does the healing. Some people believe that mind-intent can be used to heal illnesses, and this has misled people. This view has to be clarified.

Human thoughts are a type of message, a type of energy, and a form of material existence. When a person thinks, the brain produces a frequency. Sometimes it is quite effective to chant a mantra. Why? It's because the universe has its own vibrational frequency, and an effect will be produced when the frequency of your mantra coincides with that of the universe. For it to be effective, it certainly has to be of a benign nature since evil things are not allowed to exist in the universe. Mind-intent is also a specific kind of thought. The Law Bodies of a high-level *qigong* grand master are controlled and dictated by the thoughts of his main body. A Law Body also has his own thoughts and his own independent ability to solve problems and carry out tasks. He is an entirely independent self. At the same time, Law Bodies know the thoughts of the *qigong* master's main body and will carry out tasks according to those thoughts. For example, if the *qigong* master wants to treat a particular person's illness, Law Bodies will go there. Without that thought they will not go. When they see an extremely good thing to do they will do it on their own. Some masters haven't achieved Enlightenment, and there are things that they still don't know but that their Law Bodies already know.

"Mind-intent" also has another meaning, namely, inspiration. Inspiration doesn't come from one's Main Consciousness. The knowledge base of the Main Consciousness is quite limited. It won't work if you depend solely on the Main Consciousness to come up with something that doesn't yet exist in this society.

[47] Dafa (dah-fah)—"The Great Way," or "The Great Law"; short for the name Falun Dafa, "The Great (Cultivation) Way of the Law Wheel."

Inspiration comes from the Assistant Consciousness. When some people engaged in creative work or scientific research get stuck after exhausting all of their brainpower, they put things aside, rest for a while, or take a walk outside. Inspiration then comes suddenly without their thinking. They immediately start to write everything down quickly, thereby creating something. This is because when the Main Consciousness is strong, it controls the brain and nothing will come forth, despite its effort. Once the Main Consciousness relaxes, the Assistant Consciousness starts to function and control the brain. The Assistant Consciousness is able to create new things, as it belongs to another dimension and is unrestrained by this one. Yet the Assistant Consciousness can't surpass or interfere with the state of human society; it isn't allowed to affect the process of society's development.

Inspiration comes from two sources. One is the Assistant Consciousness. The Assistant Consciousness isn't deluded by this world and can produce inspiration. The other source is the command and guidance from high-level beings. When guided by high-level beings, people's minds are expanded and able to create groundbreaking things. The entire development of society and the universe follow their own specific laws. Nothing happens by chance.

6. Levels of Cultivation in Falun Gong

(1) Cultivation at High Levels

Since Falun Gong cultivation takes place at really high levels, *gong* is generated quite rapidly. A great cultivation way is extremely simple and easy. Falun Gong has few movements. Yet viewed from a larger scope it governs all aspects of the body, including the many things that are to be generated. As long as a person's *xinxing* keeps rising, his or her *gong* will grow rapidly; there is little need for intention-filled effort, the use of any specific method, setting up a crucible and furnace to make elixir from gathered chemicals or from adding fire and gathered chemicals. Relying on the guidance of mind-intent can be rather complicated and can make it easy for one to go awry. Here we provide the most convenient and best cultivation way, yet also the most difficult one. In order for a cultivator to reach the Milk-White Body state using other methods, it would take more than a decade, several decades, or even longer. Yet we bring you to this stage immediately. This level might already pass by before you even feel it. It might only last several hours. There will be one day when you feel quite sensitive, and only a little while later you won't feel as sensitive. In fact, you will have just passed a significant level.

(2) Manifestations of Gong

After students of Falun Gong go through adjustment of the flesh body, they will reach the state that is suitable for Dafa[47] cultivation: the Milk-White Body state. *Gong* will only develop after this state is reached. People with a high-level Third Eye can see that *gong* develops on the surface of a practitioner's skin and is then absorbed into his or her body. This process of *gong* generation and absorption keeps repeating itself, going level after level, sometimes really rapidly. This is first-round *gong*. After the first round, the body of the practitioner is no longer a regular one. A practitioner will never again get sick after reaching the Milk-White Body state. The pain that might emerge here and there or the discomfort in a certain area is not sickness, though it might appear to be similar: It is caused by karma. After the second round of *gong* development, one's intelligent beings will have grown very large and are able to move around and talk. Sometimes they are produced sparsely, sometimes in great density. They can talk to one another. There is a great deal of energy stored in those intelligent beings, and this is used to change one's original-body.

At a certain advanced level in Falun Gong cultivation, Cultivated Infants (*yinghai*) sometimes appear all throughout a practitioner's body. They are mischievous, enjoy playing, and are kindhearted. Another kind of body can also be produced: the Immortal Infant (*yuanying*). He or she sits on a lotus flower throne that is very beautiful. The Immortal Infant generated through cultivation is created by the merging of *yin* and *yang* within the human body. Both male and female cultivators are able to cultivate an Immortal Infant. At the beginning the Immortal Infant is very small. He gradually grows larger and ultimately grows to be the cultivator's size. He looks exactly like the cultivator and is indeed present there in the cultivator's body. When people with supernormal abilities look at him or her, they will say that this person has two bodies. Actually, this person has succeeded in cultivating his or her true body. Many Law Bodies can also be developed through cultivation. In short, all supernormal abilities that can be developed in the universe can be developed in Falun Gong; supernormal abilities developed in other cultivation methods are also all included in Falun Gong.

(3) Beyond-Triple-World-Law Cultivation

By performing Falun Gong exercises, practitioners can make their meridians wider and wider, connecting them to become one piece. That is, a person cultivates to a state in which there are no meridians or acupuncture points, or conversely, meridians and acupuncture points exist everywhere. This still doesn't mean that he or she has attained the Dao—it is only one type of manifestation in the process of Falun Gong cultivation and the reflection of one level. When this

53

stage is reached, the person is at the end of In-Triple-World-Law cultivation. The *gong* he or she has developed will already be quite powerful and will have finished taking shape. Also, this person's *gong* column will be really high and the three flowers will appear atop his or her head. By that time this person will have merely taken the last step of In-Triple-World-Law cultivation.

When another step forward is taken, there will be nothing left. All of the person's supernormal abilities will be pressed into the body's deepest dimension. He or she will enter the Pure-White Body state, wherein the body is transparent. With one more step forward, this person will enter into Beyond-Triple-World-Law cultivation, also known as "cultivation of a Buddha's body." The supernormal abilities developed at this stage belong to the category of divine powers. The practitioner will have unlimited powers at this point and will have become incredibly mighty. Upon reaching higher realms, he or she will cultivate to become a great enlightened being. All of this depends on how you cultivate your *xinxing*. Whichever level you cultivate to is the level of your Attainment Status. Dedicated cultivators find a righteous cultivation way and achieve Righteous Attainment—this is Consummation.

Chapter III
Cultivation of Xinxing

All cultivators of Falun Gong must make cultivation of *xinxing* their top priority and regard *xinxing* as the key to developing *gong*. This is the principle for cultivating at high levels. Strictly speaking, the *gong* potency that determines one's level isn't developed through performing exercises but through *xinxing* cultivation. Improving *xinxing* is easier said than done. Cultivators must be able to put forth great effort, improve their enlightenment quality, bear hardships upon hardships, endure almost unendurable things, and so on. Why haven't some people's *gong* grown even though they have practiced for years? The fundamental causes are: first, they disregard *xinxing*; second, they do not know a high-level righteous cultivation way. This point must be brought to light. Many masters who teach a practice system talk about *xinxing*—they are teaching genuine things. Those who only teach movements and techniques without ever discussing *xinxing* are actually teaching wicked cultivation. So practitioners have to exert great effort in improving their *xinxing* before they can start cultivation at higher levels.

1. Xinxing's Inner Meaning

The "*xinxing*" referred to in Falun Gong cannot be fully encompassed by "virtue" alone. It encompasses much more than virtue. It encompasses many different facets of things, including those of virtue. Virtue is only one manifestation of one's *xinxing*, so using only virtue to understand the meaning of *xinxing* is

55

inadequate. *Xinxing* encompasses how to deal with the two matters of gain and loss. "Gain" is to gain conformity to the nature of the universe. The nature that comprises the universe is Zhen-Shan-Ren. A cultivator's degree of conformity to the nature of the universe is reflected in the amount of his or her virtue. "Loss" is to abandon negative thoughts and behaviors, such as greed, the pursuit of personal gain, lust, desire, killing, fighting, theft, robbery, deception, jealousy, etc. If one is to cultivate to high levels, one also needs to break with the pursuit of desires, something inherent in humans. In other words, one should let go of all attachments and take lightly all matters of personal gain and reputation.

A complete person is composed of a flesh body and character. The same is true with the universe: In addition to the existence of substances, there also simultaneously exists the nature Zhen-Shan-Ren. Every particle of air contains this nature. This nature is made manifest in human society in the fact that good actions are met with rewards and bad ones with punishment. At a high level this nature also manifests as supernormal abilities. People who align themselves with this nature are good people; those who depart from it are bad. People who comply with it and assimilate to it are those who attain the Dao. In order to conform to this nature, practitioners need to have extremely high *xinxing*. Only this way can one cultivate to high levels.

It is easy to be a good person, but it is not easy to cultivate *xinxing*—cultivators must prepare mentally. Sincerity is a prerequisite if you are to rectify your heart. People live in this world in which society has become rather complicated. Though you want to do good deeds, there are some people who don't want you to; you do not want to harm others, but others might harm you for various reasons. Some of these things happen for unnatural reasons. Will you understand the reasons? What should

56

you do? The struggles in this world test your xinxing at every moment. When confronted with indescribable humiliation, when your vested interests are infringed upon, when faced with money and lust, when in a power struggle, when rage and jealousy emerge in conflicts, when various types of discord in society and in the family take place, and when all kinds of suffering occur, can you always handle yourself in accordance with the strict *xinxing* criteria? Of course, if you can handle everything you are already an enlightened being. Most practitioners start as everyday people after all, and cultivation of *xinxing* is gradual; it moves upward little by little. Determined cultivators will eventually gain Righteous Attainment if they are prepared to endure great hardships and to face difficulties with a firm mind. I hope that each of you cultivators maintains your *xinxing* well and improves your *gong* potency rapidly!

2. Loss and Gain

Both *qigong* and religious circles talk about loss and gain. Some people take "loss" to mean being charitable, doing some good deeds, or giving a hand to people in need, and "gain" to mean gaining *gong*. Even monks in temples also say that one should be charitable. This understanding narrows the meaning of loss. The loss we talk about is much broader—it's something of a larger scale. The things we require you to lose are the attachments of everyday people and the mindset that doesn't let go of those attachments. If you can break with the things you consider important and part with the things you think you can't part with, that is loss in the truest sense. Offering help and displays of charity are only a part of loss.

An everyday person wants to enjoy renown, personal gain, a better standard of living, more comfort, and more money. These are everyday people's goals. As practitioners, we are different, for what we acquire is *gong*, not those things. We need to care less about personal gain and take it lightly, but we are not really asked to lose any material things; we cultivate in human society and need to live as everyday people do. The key is for you to break your attachments—you aren't really required to lose anything. Whatever belongs to you won't be lost, while the things that don't belong to you cannot be acquired. If they are acquired they will have to be returned to others. To gain, you must lose. Of course, it's impossible to immediately handle everything very well, just as it's impossible to become an enlightened being overnight. Yet by cultivating little by little and improving step by step, it is attainable. You will gain however much you lose. You should always take matters of personal gain lightly and prefer to gain less in order to have peace of mind. When it comes to material things you might suffer some losses, but you will gain in terms of virtue and *gong*. Herein lies the truth. You are not to intentionally gain virtue and *gong* by exchanging your renown, money, and personal gain. This should be understood further using your enlightenment quality.

Someone who cultivated in a high-level Daoist practice once said: "I don't want the things others want, and I don't possess the things others possess; but I have things others don't, and I want things others don't." An everyday person hardly has a moment when he or she feels satisfied. This kind of person wants everything except the rocks lying on the ground that no one wants

---

[48] Lao Zi (laow dzz)—author of the *Dao De Jing* and popularly regarded as the founder of Daoism, Lao Zi is thought to have lived sometime around the 4th century BC. Note: *Dao De Jing* is sometimes romanized as *Tao Te Ching*.

to pick up. Yet this Daoist cultivator said, "Then I'll pick up those rocks." A proverb goes like this: "Rarity makes something precious, scarcity makes something unique." Rocks are worthless here but could be most valuable in other dimensions. This is a principle that an everyday person can't understand. Many enlightened, high-level masters with great virtue have no material possessions. For them, there is nothing that cannot be given up.

The path of cultivation is the most correct one, and practitioners are actually the most intelligent people. The things that everyday people struggle for and the minute benefits they gain only last a short while. Even if you obtain through struggling, find something for free, or profit a little, so what? There is a saying among everyday people: "You can't bring anything with you when you are born, and you can't take anything away with you when you die." You enter the world having nothing, and you take away nothing when you leave it—even your bones will be burned to ashes. It doesn't matter if you have tons of money or are a dignitary—nothing can be taken with you when you leave. Yet since *gong* grows on the body of your Main Consciousness, it can be taken forth. I am telling you that *gong* is hard to earn. It is so precious and so hard to acquire that it can't be exchanged for any amount of money. Once your *gong* has reached an advanced level, should you one day decide not to cultivate anymore, as long as you don't do anything bad, your *gong* will be converted into any material thing you want—you will be able to have them all. But you will no longer have the things that cultivators possess. You will instead have only the things that one can acquire in this world.

Self-interest leads some people to use improper means to take things that belong to others. These people think that they get a good deal. The truth is that they gain that profit by exchanging their virtue with others—only they don't know it. For a practitioner, this would have to be deducted from his or her *gong*. For a nonpractitioner, it would have to be deducted from his or her life expectancy or from something else. In short, the books will be balanced. This is the principle of the universe. There are also some people who always mistreat others, harm others with abusive words, and so on. With these actions they throw a corresponding portion of their virtue to the other party, exchanging their virtue for the act of insulting others.

Some people think it's disadvantageous to be a good person. From an everyday person's viewpoint, a good person is at a disadvantage. But what they acquire is something that everyday people cannot: virtue, a white substance that is extremely precious. Without virtue one cannot have *gong*—this is an absolute truth. Why is it that many people cultivate but their *gong* fails to develop? It is precisely because they don't cultivate virtue. Many people emphasize virtue and require cultivation of virtue, yet they fail to disclose the real principles of how virtue is evolved into *gong*. It is left for the individual to comprehend. The close to ten thousand volumes of the *Tripitaka* and the principles that Sakyamuni taught for over forty-some years all talked about one thing: virtue. The ancient Chinese books of Daoist cultivation all discuss virtue. The five-thousand-word book by Lao Zi,[48] *Dao De Jing*, also contemplates virtue (*de*). Some people still fail to understand this.

We talk about "loss." When you gain, you must lose. You will encounter some tribulations when you genuinely want to cultivate. When they manifest in your life, you might experience a little

---

[49] Ah Q (ah cue)—a foolish character in a well-known Chinese novel.

[50] Han Xin (hahn shin)—a leading general for Liu Bang, the first emperor of the Han Dynasty (206 B.C. - 23 A.D.).

bodily suffering or feel uncomfortable here or there—but it's not sickness. The hardships can also manifest in society, in the family, or in the workplace—anything is possible. Discord will suddenly arise over personal gain or emotional tensions. The goal is to enable you to improve your *xinxing*. These things usually happen suddenly and seem extremely intense. If you encounter something that is very tricky, embarrassing for you, that makes you lose face, or puts you in an awkward position, how are you going to handle it at that point? If you stay calm and unruffled—if you're able to do that—your *xinxing* will be improved through the tribulation and your *gong* will develop proportionately. If you can achieve a little, you will gain a little. However much you expend is however much you gain. Typically, when we are in the middle of a tribulation we might not be able to realize this, yet we have to try. We shouldn't regard ourselves as everyday people. We should hold ourselves to higher standards when discord arises. Our *xinxing* will be tempered among everyday people since we cultivate amidst them. We are bound to make some mistakes and to learn something from these. It's impossible for your *gong* to develop while you are comfortable and not encountering any problems.

3. Simultaneous Cultivation of Zhen, Shan, and Ren

Our cultivation way cultivates Zhen, Shan, and Ren simultaneously. "Zhen" is about telling the truth, doing truthful things, returning to one's origin and true self, and ultimately becoming a true person. "Shan" is about developing great compassion, doing good things, and saving people. We particularly emphasize the ability of Ren. Only with Ren can one cultivate to become a person with great virtue. Ren is a very powerful thing and transcends Zhen and Shan. Throughout the entire cultivation process you are asked to forbear, to watch your *xinxing*, and to exercise self-control.

It's not easy to forbear when confronted with problems. Some say, "If you don't hit back when beaten, don't talk back when slandered, or if you forbear even when you lose face in front of your family, relatives, and good friends, haven't you turned into Ah Q?!"[49] I say that if you act normal in all regards, if your intelligence is no less than that of others, and if it's only that you have taken lightly the matter of personal gain, no one is going to say you are foolish. Being able to forbear is not weakness, and neither is it being like Ah Q. It is a display of strong will and self-restraint. There was a person in Chinese history named Han Xin[50] who once suffered the humiliation of crawling between someone's legs. That was great forbearance. There is an ancient saying: "When an everyday person is humiliated, he will draw his sword to fight." It means that when a common person is humiliated, he will draw his sword to retaliate, will swear at others, or will throw punches at them. It's not an easy thing for a person to come and live a lifetime. Some people live for their ego—it's not worth it whatsoever, and it is also extremely tiring. There is a saying in China: "With one step back, you will discover a boundless sea and sky." Take a step back when you are confronted with troubles, and you will find a whole different scenario.

A practitioner should not only show forbearance towards the people with whom he has conflicts and those who embarrass him directly, but should also adopt a generous attitude and even thank them. How could you improve your *xinxing* if it weren't for your difficulties with them? How could the black substance be transformed into the white substance during suffering? How could you develop

62

your *gong*? It is very difficult when you are in the midst of a tribulation, yet you must exercise self-restraint at that point. The tribulations will get continually stronger as your *gong* potency increases. Everything depends on whether you can improve your *xinxing*. That tribulation might be upsetting to you at the beginning and make you unbearably angry—so angry that your veins bulge. Yet you don't erupt and you are able to contain your anger— that's good. You have started to forbear, to intentionally forbear. You will then gradually and continuously improve your *xinxing*, truly taking these things lightly; that is an even greater improvement. Everyday people take insignificant friction and minor problems really seriously. They live for their ego and tolerate nothing. They will dare to do anything when they are angered to an unbearable point. Yet as a practitioner you will find the things that people take seriously to be very, very trivial— even too trivial—because your goal is extremely long-term and far-reaching. You will live as long as this universe. Then think about those things again: It doesn't matter if you have them or not. You can put them all behind you when you think from a broader perspective.

4. Eliminating Jealousy

Jealousy is a huge obstacle in cultivation and one that has a large impact on practitioners. It directly impacts a practitioner's *gong* potency, harms fellow cultivators, and seriously interferes with our ascension in cultivation. As a practitioner, you have to eliminate it one hundred percent. Some people have yet to forgo jealousy even though they have cultivated to a certain level. Moreover, the harder it is to abandon, the easier it is for jealousy to grow stronger. The negative

63

effects of this attachment make the improved parts of one's *xinxing* vulnerable. Why is jealousy being singled out for discussion? It's because jealousy is the strongest, most prominent thing that manifests among Chinese people; it weighs most heavily in people's thinking. Many people are nonetheless unaware of it. Called Oriental jealousy, or Asian jealousy, it is characteristic of the East. The Chinese people are quite introverted, reserved, and don't express themselves openly. All of this easily leads to jealousy. Everything has two sides. Accordingly, an introverted personality has its pros and cons. Westerners are relatively extroverted. For example, a child who scored a one hundred in school might happily call out on his way home, "I got a hundred!" Neighbors would open their doors and windows to congratulate him, "Congratulations, Tom!" All of them would be happy for him. If this happened in China—think about it—people would feel disgusted once they heard it: "He scored a hundred. So what? What's there to show off about?" The reaction is completely different when one has a jealous mentality.

Jealous types look down upon others and don't allow others to surpass them. When they see someone more capable than they, their minds lose all perspective, they find it unbearable, and they deny the fact. They want to get pay raises when others do, get equal bonuses, and share the same burden when something goes wrong. They get green-eyed and jealous when they see others making more money. At any rate, they find it unacceptable if others do better than they. Some people are afraid of accepting a bonus when they have made certain achievements in their scientific research; they are afraid of others becoming jealous. Some people who have been awarded certain honors don't dare reveal them for fear of jealousy and sarcasm. Some *qigong* masters can't stand to see other *qigong* masters teach, so they go make trouble for them. This is a *xinxing* problem. Suppose that in a group that does *qigong* exercises together, some people who started later are nonetheless the first persons to develop supernormal abilities. There are people who would then say: "What's he got to brag about? I've practiced for so many years and have a huge pile of certificates. How could he develop supernormal abilities before me?" His jealousy would then emerge. Cultivation focuses inward, and a cultivator should cultivate him or herself and look within to find the source of problems. You should work hard on yourself and try to improve in the areas you haven't done enough with. If you look hard at others to find the source of friction, others will succeed in cultivation and ascend, while you will be the only one left here. Won't you have wasted all of your time? Cultivation is for cultivating oneself!

Jealousy also harms fellow cultivators, such as when one's badmouthing makes it hard for others to enter tranquility. When this type of person has supernormal abilities, he or she might use them out of jealousy to harm fellow cultivators. For example, a person sits there meditating, and he has been cultivating fairly well. He sits there like a mountain since he has *gong*. Then two beings float by, one of who used to be a monk but who, due to jealousy, didn't achieve Enlightenment; even though he possesses a certain *gong* potency, he has not reached Consummation. When they arrive at where the person is meditating, one says, "So-and-so is meditating here. Let's go around him." Yet the other says, "In the past, I chopped off a corner of Mount Tai." He then tries to strike the practitioner. But when he raises his hand he can't bring it down. That being is unable to strike the practitioner because he is cultivating in a righteous practice and has a protective shield. He wants to harm someone who cultivates a righteous way, so it becomes a serious matter and he will be punished. People who are jealous harm themselves as well as others.

5. Eliminating Attachments

"Having attachments" refers to the relentless, zealous pursuit of a particular object or goal by those practitioners who are unable to liberate themselves or too stubborn to heed any advice. Some people pursue supernormal abilities in this world, and this will certainly impact their cultivating to high levels. The stronger the feelings, the more difficult they are to abandon. Their minds will become ever more unbalanced and unstable. Later on these people will feel that they have gained nothing, and they will even start to doubt the things that they have been learning. Attachments stem from human desires. The characteristics of attachments are that their targets or goals are obviously limited, fairly clear and particular, and frequently the person might be unaware of the attachments. An everyday person has many attachments. He might use any means necessary in order to pursue something and obtain it. A cultivator's attachments manifest differently, such as in his pursuing a particular supernormal ability, his indulging in a certain vision, his obsessing over a certain phenomenon, and so on. No matter what you, a practitioner, pursue, it is incorrect—pursuit has to be abandoned. The Dao School teaches nothingness. The Buddha School teaches emptiness and how to enter the gate of emptiness. We ultimately want to achieve the state of nothingness and emptiness, letting go of every attachment. Anything that you cannot let go of has to be discarded. The pursuit of supernormal abilities is an example: If you pursue them it means you want to use them. In reality, that is going against the nature of our universe. It is actually still an issue of *xinxing*. You want to have them; you just want to flaunt them and show them off in front of others. Those abilities aren't something to showcase for others' viewing. Even if the purposes of your using them were innocent and you just wanted to use them to do some good deeds, the good deeds that you did could turn out to be not so good. It's not necessarily a good idea to handle matters of everyday people using supernormal means. After some people hear me remark that seventy percent of the class has had the Third Eye opened, they start to wonder, "Why can't I sense anything?" Their attention focuses on the Third Eye when they return home and do the exercises—even to the point of getting a headache. They still can't see anything in the end. This is an attachment. Individuals differ in physical state of being and inborn quality. It isn't possible that all of them come to see through the Third Eye at the same time, and neither can each person's Third Eye be at the same level. Some people might be able to see and some might not. It is all normal.

Attachments can bring the development of a cultivator's *gong* potency to a grinding halt. In more serious cases they might even result in practitioners taking a wicked path. In particular, certain supernormal abilities might be used by people with inferior *xinxing* to do bad things. There have been cases in which a person's unreliable *xinxing* has resulted in supernormal abilities being used to commit bad deeds. Somewhere there was a male college student who developed the supernormal ability of mind control. With this he could use his own thoughts to manipulate the thoughts and conduct of others, and he used his ability to do bad things. Some people might witness visions appearing when they do the exercises. They always want to have a clear look and full understanding. This is also a form of attachment. A certain hobby might become an addiction for some, and they are unable to shake it. That, too, is a form of attachment. Because of differences in inborn quality and intentions, some people cultivate in order to reach the highest level while some cultivate just to gain certain things. The latter mentality surely limits the goal of one's cultivation. If a person doesn't eliminate this kind of attachment, his or her *gong* won't develop even through practicing. So practitioners should take all material gains lightly, pursue nothing, and let everything unfold naturally, thus avoiding the emergence of new attachments. Whether this can be done depends upon a practitioner's *xinxing*. One cannot succeed in cultivation if one's *xinxing* isn't fundamentally changed or if any attachments remain.

6. Karma

(1) The Origin of Karma

Karma is a type of black substance that is the opposite of virtue. In Buddhism it is called sinful karma, while here we call it karma. So doing bad things is called producing karma. Karma is produced by a person's doing wrong in this life or in past lives. For instance, killing, taking advantage of others, infringing upon others' interests, gossiping about someone behind his or her back, being unfriendly to someone, and so on can all create karma. In addition, some karma is passed on from ancestors, family and relatives, or close friends. When one throws punches at someone else, one also throws one's white substance over to the other person, and the vacated area in one's body is then filled with the black substance. Killing is the worst evildoing—it is a wrongdoing and will generate heavy karma. Karma is the primary factor causing sickness in people. Of course, it doesn't always manifest itself in the form of sickness—it can also manifest as encountering some difficulties and the like. All of these things are karma at work. So practitioners must not do anything bad. Any misconduct will produce negative influences that will seriously impact your cultivation.

Some people encourage collecting the *qi* of plants. When they teach their exercises they also teach how to collect *qi* from plants; they discuss with intense interest which trees have better *qi* and the colors of different trees' *qi*. There were some people in a park in our northeastern region who practiced a kind of so-called *qigong* in which they would roll all over the ground. After getting up, they would circle around the pine trees to collect their *qi*. Within half a year the grove of pine trees had withered and turned yellow. This was a karma-generating act! It too was killing! Collecting *qi* from plants is not right, whether it's viewed in light of our country's greening, the maintenance of ecological balance, or from a high-level perspective. The universe is vast and boundless, with *qi* available everywhere for you to collect. Knock yourself out and go collect it—why abuse these plants? If you are a practitioner, where is your heart of mercy and compassion?

Everything has intelligence. Modern science already recognizes that plants have not only life, but also intelligence, thoughts, feelings, and even super-sensory functions. When your Third Eye reaches the level of Law Eyesight, you will discover that the world is a totally different place. When you go outside, rocks, walls, and even trees will talk to you. All objects have life. No sooner does an object form than a life enters it. It is people living on Earth who categorize substances as organic and inorganic. People living in temples get upset when they break a bowl, for the moment it is destroyed, its living entity is released. It hasn't finished its life journey, so it will have nowhere to go. It will therefore have extreme hatred towards the person who ended its life. The angrier it gets, the more karma the person will accrue. Some "*qigong* masters" even go hunting. Where did their benevolence and compassion go? The Buddha and Dao Schools don't do things that violate heaven's principles. When one does these things, it is an act of killing.

Some people say that in the past they produced a lot of karma, for example, by killing fish or chickens, by fishing, etc. Does this mean that they can no longer cultivate? No, it does not. Back then, you did it without knowing the consequences, so it wouldn't have created extra karma. Just don't do it anymore in the future, and that should be fine. If you do it again you will be knowingly violating the principles, and that is not permitted. Some of our practitioners have this kind of karma. Your attendance at our seminar means that you have a predestined relationship, and that you can cultivate upward. Shall we swat flies or mosquitoes when they come inside? As to your handling of this at your present level, it isn't considered wrong if you swat and kill them. If you cannot drive them out, then killing them is no big deal. When the time has come for something to die, naturally it will die. Once, when Sakyamuni was still alive, he wanted to take a bath and asked his disciple to clean the bathtub. The disciple discovered many bugs in the bathtub, so he returned and asked what he should do. Sakyamuni said it again, "It is the bathtub that I want you to clean." The disciple understood, and he went back and cleaned the bathtub. You shouldn't take certain things too seriously. We don't intend to make you an overly cautious person. In a complicated environment it is not right, I think, if you are nervous at every moment and afraid of doing something wrong. It would be a form of attachment—fear itself is an attachment.

We should have a compassionate and merciful heart. When we handle things with a compassionate and merciful heart we are less likely to cause problems. Take self-interest lightly and be kindhearted, and your compassionate heart will keep you from doing wrong. Believe it or not, you will discover that if you always hold a spiteful attitude and always want to fight and contend, you will even turn good things into bad ones. I often see some people who, when right, won't let others be; when this type of person is right he has finally found some grounds for mistreating others. Similarly, we shouldn't stir up conflict if we disagree with certain things. The things you dislike might at times not necessarily be wrong. When you continuously raise your level as a practitioner, every sentence you say will carry energy. You shouldn't speak as you please, since you will be able to restrain everyday people. It is particularly easy for you to commit wrongdoing and create karma when you aren't able to see the truth of problems and their karmic causes.

(2) Eliminating Karma

The principles in this world are the same as those in heaven: Eventually you have to pay what you owe others. Even everyday people have to pay what they owe others. All the hardships and problems you encounter throughout your life result from karma. You have to pay. The path of life for us genuine cultivators will be altered. A new path that suits your cultivation will be arranged. Your master will reduce some of your karma, and what remains will be used to improve your *xinxing*. You exchange and pay for your karma through performing the exercises and through cultivating your *xinxing*. From now on, the problems you confront won't happen by chance. So please be mentally prepared. By enduring some tribulations, you will come to let go of all the things an everyday person can't release. You will run into many troubles. Problems will arise within the family, socially, and from other sources, or you might suddenly encounter disaster; it could even be that you will get blamed for what is actually someone else's fault, and so on and so forth. Practitioners aren't supposed to get sick, yet you might suddenly come down with a serious sickness. The sickness could come on with intense force, causing you to suffer to the point where you are no longer able to bear it.

Even hospital exams might yield no diagnosis. Yet for an unknown reason the sickness might later disappear without any treatment. In fact, your debts are paid in this manner. Perhaps one day your spouse will lose his or her temper and start a fight with you for no reason at all; even insignificant incidents might trigger big arguments. Afterwards, your spouse too will feel confused over his or her loss of temper. As you are a practitioner, you should be clear as to why this kind of incident takes place: It's because that "thing" came, and it was asking you to pay for your karma. To resolve these sorts of incidents, you have to keep yourself under control during those moments and watch your *xinxing*. Be appreciative and thankful that your spouse has helped you pay for your karma.

The legs will start to ache after one sits in meditation for a long while, and sometimes the pain is excruciating. People with a high-level Third Eye can see the following: When one is in great pain, there is a large chunk of the black substance—both inside and outside of the body—coming down and being eliminated. The pain one experiences while sitting in meditation is intermittent and excruciating. Some understand it and are determined not to unfold their legs. The black substance will then be eliminated and transformed into the white substance, and it will in turn be evolved into *gong*. Practitioners can't possibly pay for all of their karma through sitting in meditation and performing the exercises. They also need to improve their *xinxing* and enlightenment quality, and to undergo some tribulations. What is important is that we be compassionate. One's compassion emerges quickly in our Falun Gong. Many people find that tears start to fall for no reason while they sit in meditation. Whatever they think of, they feel grief. Whoever they look at, they see suffering. This is actually the heart of great compassion that emerges. Your nature, your genuine self, will start to connect with

72

the nature of the universe: Zhen-Shan-Ren. When your compassionate nature emerges, you will do things with much kindness. From your inner heart to your outer appearance, everyone will be able to see that you are really kind. At that point no one will mistreat you anymore. If someone were to treat you unfairly then, your heart of great compassion would be at play and you wouldn't do the same to him in return. This is a type of power, a power that makes you different from everyday people.

When you encounter a tribulation, that great compassion will help you overcome it. At the same time, my Law Bodies will look after you and protect your life, but you will have to undergo the tribulation. For example, when I was lecturing in Taiyuan there was an older couple that came to attend my class. They were hurrying when they crossed the street, and upon reaching the middle of the road a car came speeding along. It instantly knocked the elderly woman down and dragged her along for more than ten meters before she finally fell in the middle of the street. The car couldn't stop for another twenty meters. The driver got out of the car and said some rude words, and the passengers sitting inside the car also uttered some negative things. At that moment the elderly woman remembered what I had said and didn't say anything. After she got up, she said, "Everything is all right, nothing is broken." She then went into the lecture hall with her husband. Had she said at that very moment, "Oh, it hurts here and it hurts there, too. You need to take me to the hospital," things would have turned out really badly. But she didn't say that. The elderly woman said to me: "Master, I know what that was all about. It was helping me pay for my karma!" A great tribulation was eliminated and a big chunk of karma was removed. As you can imagine, she had really high *xinxing* and good enlightenment quality. She was that elderly, the car was travelling that fast, and she was dragged that far before finally hitting the ground hard—yet she got up having a right mind.

Sometimes a tribulation seems tremendous when it comes—so overwhelming that there looks to be no way out. Perhaps it stays around for quite a few days. Then a path suddenly appears and things start to take a huge turn. In fact, it's because we have improved our *xinxing* and the problem has disappeared naturally.

In order to improve your realm of mind, you have to be tested by various tribulations in this world. If your *xinxing* has really improved and stabilized, karma will be eliminated during the process, the tribulation will pass, and your *gong* will develop. Don't be discouraged if during *xinxing* tests you fail to watch your *xinxing* and you conduct yourself improperly. Take the initiative to find what you learned from this lesson, to discover where you fell short, and to put effort into cultivating Zhen-Shan-Ren. The next problem that will test your *xinxing* might come shortly thereafter. As your *gong* potency develops, the next tribulation's test might come on even stronger and more suddenly. Your *gong* potency will grow a little bit higher with every problem you overcome. The development of your *gong* will come to a standstill if you are unable to overcome a problem. Small tests lead to small improvements; big tests lead to big improvements. I hope that every practitioner is prepared to endure great suffering and will have the determination and willpower to embrace hardships. You won't acquire real *gong* without expending effort. There is no principle in existence that will let you gain *gong* comfortably without any suffering or effort. You will never cultivate to become an enlightened being if your *xinxing* doesn't become fundamentally better and you still harbor personal attachments!

7. Demonic Interference

"Demonic interference" refers to the manifestations or visions that appear during the cultivation process and that interfere with a person's practice. Their goal is to prevent practitioners from cultivating to high levels. In other words, demons come to collect debts.

The problem of demonic interference will surely arise when a person is cultivating to high levels. It's impossible that one has not committed wrongdoing in one's lifetime, just as one's ancestors must have in their lives; this is called karma. Whether a person's inborn quality is good or not reflects how much karma this person carries with him or her. Even if he or she is a rather good person it is still impossible to be free of karma. You can't sense it because you don't practice cultivation. Demons won't care if your practice is only for healing and improving health. But they will bother you once you begin cultivating to high levels. They can disturb you using many different methods, the goal of which is to prevent you from cultivating to high levels and to make you fail in your practice. Demons manifest themselves in a variety of ways. Some manifest themselves as daily life happenings, while others take the form of phenomena from other dimensions. They command things to interfere with you every time you sit down to meditate, making it impossible for you to enter tranquility and, therefore, to cultivate to high levels. Sometimes the moment you sit down to meditate you will begin to doze off or will have all kinds of thoughts going through your mind, and you become unable to enter into a cultivation state. At other times, the moment you start to perform the exercises, your once-quiet surroundings will suddenly be filled with the noise of footsteps, doors slamming, cars honking, telephones ringing, and a variety of other forms of interference, making it impossible for you to become tranquil.

Another kind of demon is sexual lust. A beautiful woman or handsome man might appear in front of a practitioner during his or her meditation or dreams. That person will entice you and seduce you by making stimulating gestures that evoke your attachment to sexual lust. If you can't overcome this the first time, it will gradually escalate and continue to seduce you until you abandon the idea of cultivating to a high level. This is a difficult test to pass, and quite a few practitioners have failed because of this. I hope you are mentally prepared for it. If someone doesn't guard his or her *xinxing* well enough and fails the first time, he or she should truly learn a lesson from it. It will come again and interfere many times until you truly maintain your *xinxing* and completely break that attachment. This is a big hurdle that you must overcome, or you will be unable to attain the Dao and succeed in cultivation.

There is another kind of demon that also presents itself during one's performance of the exercises or in one's dreams. Some people suddenly see some horrifying faces that are ugly and real, or figures that are holding knives and threatening to kill. But they can only scare people. If they were to really stab, they wouldn't be able to touch the practitioner since Master has installed a protective shield around the practitioner's body to keep him or her unharmed. They try to scare the person off so that he or she will stop cultivating. These only appear at a certain level or during a certain period of time and will pass quickly—in a few days, a week, or a few weeks. It all depends on how high your *xinxing* is and how you treat this matter.

8. Inborn Quality and Enlightenment Quality

"Inborn quality" refers to the white substance one brings with oneself at birth. In fact, it is virtue—a tangible substance. The more of this substance you bring with you, the better your inborn quality. People with good inborn quality more easily return to their true self and become enlightened, as their thinking is unimpeded. Once they hear about learning *qigong* or about things concerning cultivation, they immediately become interested and are willing to learn. They can connect with the universe. It is exactly as Lao Zi said: "When a wise man hears the Dao, he will practice it diligently. When an average man hears it, he will practice it on and off. When a foolish man hears it, he will laugh at it loudly. If he doesn't laugh loudly, it is not the Dao." Those people who can easily return to their true self and become enlightened are wise people. In contrast, a person with a lot of the black substance and an inferior inborn quality has a barrier formed outside of his body that makes it impossible for him to accept good things. The black substance will make him disbelieve good things when he encounters them. In fact, this is one of the roles karma plays.

A discussion of inborn quality has to include the matter of enlightenment quality. When we talk about enlightenment, some people think that being enlightened is the equivalent of being clever. The "clever" or "cunning" person that everyday people refer to is actually far away from the cultivation practice we are discussing. These types of "clever" people usually can't achieve Enlightenment easily. They are only concerned with the practical, material world so that they can avoid being taken advantage of and avoid giving up any benefit. Most notably, a few individuals out there who regard themselves as knowledgeable, educated, and smart, think that practicing cultivation is the stuff of fairy tales. Practicing cultivation and improving *xinxing* are inconceivable to them. They consider practitioners foolish and superstitious. The enlightenment we speak of doesn't refer to being smart but to the return of human nature to its true nature, to being a good person, and to conforming to the nature of the universe. One's inborn quality determines one's enlightenment quality. If one's inborn quality is good, one's enlightenment quality tends to be good as well. Inborn quality determines enlightenment quality; however, enlightenment quality isn't entirely dictated by inborn quality. No matter how good your inborn quality is, your understanding or comprehension cannot be lacking. The inborn quality of some individuals isn't so good, yet they possess superb enlightenment quality and so can cultivate to a high level. Since we offer salvation to all sentient beings, we look at enlightenment quality, not inborn quality. Even though you have many negative things, as long as you are determined to ascend in cultivation, this thought of yours is a righteous one. With this thought you only need to forgo a little more than others and you will eventually achieve Enlightenment.

The bodies of practitioners are purified. They won't contract illness after *gong* develops, because the presence of this high-energy substance in the body no longer permits the presence of the black substance. Yet some people just refuse to believe this and always think that they are sick. They complain, "Why am I so uncomfortable?" We say that what you have gained is *gong*. How can you not have discomfort when you've gained such a good thing? In cultivation one has to give things up in an exchange. In fact, all of the discomfort is on the surface and has no impact whatsoever on your body. It appears to be sickness but it's certainly not—it all depends on whether you can awaken to this. Practitioners not only need to be able to bear the worst suffering, but they also need to have good enlightenment quality. Some people don't even try to comprehend things when they are confronted with troubles. They still treat themselves as everyday people despite my teaching them at a high level and showing them how to measure themselves with higher criteria. They can't even bring themselves to practice cultivation as genuine practitioners. Neither can they believe that they will be at a high level.

The enlightenment discussed at high levels refers to becoming enlightened, and it is categorized into Sudden Enlightenment and Gradual Enlightenment. Sudden Enlightenment refers to having the entire process of cultivation take place in a locked mode. At the last moment after you have completed the entire cultivation process and your *xinxing* has reached a high level, all of your supernormal abilities will be unlocked at once, your Third Eye will instantly open to its highest level, and your mind will be able to communicate with high-level beings in other dimensions. You will instantly be able to see the reality of the entire cosmos and its different dimensions and unitary paradises, and you will then be able to communicate with them. You will also be able to use your great divine powers. The path of sudden Enlightenment is the most difficult one to take. Throughout history, only people with superb inborn quality have been selected to become disciples; it has been passed on privately and individually. Average people would find it unbearable! The path I took was that of Sudden Enlightenment.

The things I am imparting to you belong to the path of Gradual Enlightenment. Supernormal abilities will develop in due time during your cultivation process. But the supernormal abilities that emerge will not necessarily be available for you to use, as it is easy for you to commit wrongdoing when you have not raised your *xinxing* to a certain level and are still unable to handle yourself properly. You won't be able to use these supernormal abilities for the time being, though they will eventually be made available to you. Through practicing cultivation you will gradually improve your level and come to understand the truth of this universe. Just as with Sudden Enlightenment, you will eventually reach Consummation. The path of Gradual Enlightenment is a little easier and takes no risks. What's difficult about it is that you can see the entire cultivation process. So the demands you place upon yourself should be even stricter.

9. A Clear and Pure Mind

Some people can't achieve tranquility when they do *qigong* exercises, and so they search for a method. Some have asked me: "Master, why can't I become tranquil when I perform *qigong* exercises? Can you teach me a method or technique so that I can become tranquil when I sit in meditation?" I ask, how can you become tranquil?! You still couldn't become tranquil even if a deity were to come teach you a method. Why? The reason is that your own mind isn't clear and pure. Because you live amid this society, things such as various emotions and desires, self-interest, personal matters, and even the affairs of your friends and family come to occupy your mind too much and assume a high priority. How could you become tranquil when seated in meditation? Even if you intentionally suppress them, they will still surface by themselves.

Buddhism's cultivation teaches "precept, *samadhi*, and wisdom." Precepts are for letting go of the things that you are attached to. Some Buddhists adopt the approach of chanting a Buddha's name, which requires concentrated chanting in order to achieve the state of "one thought replacing thousands of others."

80

Yet it's not simply an approach, but a type of ability. You can try chanting if you don't believe it. I can promise you that other things will arise in your mind when you use your mouth to chant a Buddha's name. It was Tibetan Tantrism that first taught people how to chant a Buddha's name; one had to chant a Buddha's name hundreds of thousands of times each day for a week. They would chant until they got dizzy and then there would finally be nothing left in their minds. That one thought had replaced all others. That is a type of skill that you might not be able to perform. There are also some other methods that teach you how to focus your mind on your *dantian*, how to count, how to fixate your eyes on objects, and so on. In actuality, none of these methods can make you enter into complete tranquility. Practitioners have to attain a clear and pure mind, discard their preoccupation with self-interest, and let go of the greed in their hearts.

Whether you can enter stillness and tranquility is in fact a reflection of your ability and level. Being able to enter tranquility the moment you sit down indicates a high level. It's all right if for the time being you can't become tranquil—you can slowly accomplish this through cultivation. Your *xinxing* improves gradually, as does your *gong*. Your *gong* will never develop unless you attach little importance to self-interest and your own desires.

Practitioners should hold themselves to higher standards at all times. Practitioners are continuously interfered with by all kinds of complicated social phenomena, many vulgar and unhealthy things, and various emotions and desires. The things that are encouraged on television, in the movies, and in literature teach you to become a stronger and more practical person among everyday people. If you can't go beyond these things you will be even further away from a cultivator's *xinxing* and state of mind, and you will acquire less *gong*. Practitioners should have little to

81

no dealings with those vulgar and unhealthy things. They should turn a blind eye and a deaf ear to them, being unmoved by people and things. I often say that the minds of everyday people cannot move me. I won't become happy when someone praises me, nor will I get upset when someone insults me. I remain unaffected no matter how serious the disruptions to *xinxing* among everyday people may be. Practitioners should take all personal gain lightly and not even care about it. Only then can your intention to become enlightened be considered mature. If you can be without strong pursuit of renown and personal gain, and even regard them as something inconsequential, you won't become frustrated or upset and your heart will always remain calm. Once you are able to let go of everything, you will naturally become clear and pure-minded.

I have taught you Dafa and all five sets of exercises. I have adjusted your bodies and installed Falun and energy mechanisms in them. My Law Bodies will protect you. All of what should be given to you has been given. During the class it's all up to me. From this point on, it's all up to you. "The master leads you through the door of cultivation, but it's up to you to continue cultivating." As long as you learn Dafa thoroughly, attentively experience and comprehend it, watch your *xinxing* at every moment, cultivate diligently, endure the worst sufferings of all, and forbear the hardships of all hardships, I believe you will surely succeed in your cultivation.

The path for cultivating *gong* lies in one's heart

The boat to sail the boundless Dafa rides on hardships

The Great Consummation Way of Falun Dafa

Movements Are the Supplementary Means for Reaching Consummation

LI HONGZHI

November 13, 1996

Chapter IV

The Characteristics of Falun Dafa

Falun Buddha Fa is a great, high-level cultivation way of the Buddha School, in which assimilation to the supreme nature of the universe, Zhen-Shan-Ren, is the foundation of cultivation practice. Its cultivation is guided by this supreme nature, and based on the principles of the universe's evolution. So what we cultivate is a Great Fa, or a Great Dao.

Falun Buddha Fa aims directly at people's hearts and makes it clear that cultivation of *xinxing* is the key to increasing *gong*. A person's *gong* level is as high as his or her *xinxing* level, and this is an absolute truth of the universe. *"Xinxing"* includes the transformation of virtue (a white substance) and *karma* (a black substance), the abandonment of ordinary human desires and attachments, and the ability to endure the toughest hardships of all. It also encompasses many types of things that a person must cultivate to raise his or her level.

Falun Buddha Fa also includes cultivation of the body, which is accomplished by performing the exercise movements of the Great Consummation Way—a great high-level practice of the Buddha School. One purpose of the exercises is to strengthen a practitioner's supernormal abilities and energy mechanisms using his or her powerful *gong* potency, thus achieving "the Fa refines the practitioner." Another purpose is to evolve many living beings in a practitioner's body. In high-level cultivation practice, the Immortal Infant or Buddha-Body will be born, and many abilities will be developed. The exercise movements are necessary for transforming and cultivating these things. The exercises are part of the harmonization and perfection in our Dafa. So Dafa is a comprehensive mind-body cultivation system. It is also called "The Great Consummation Way." This Dafa thus requires both cultivation and exercises, with cultivation taking priority over the exercises. A person's *gong* will not increase if he merely does the exercises and fails to cultivate his *xinxing*. A person who only cultivates his *xinxing* and does not perform the exercises of the Great Consummation Way will find the growth of his *gong* potency impeded and his original-body unchanged.

There are people with predestined relationships, and people who have been practicing cultivation for many years but have been unable to increase their *gong*. In order for more of them to obtain the Fa, to practice cultivation at a high level from the outset, and to increase their *gong* rapidly so as to reach Consummation directly, I have hereby imparted to the public this Dafa for cultivating Buddhahood that I cultivated and awakened to in the remote past. This cultivation way brings one to harmony and wisdom. The movements are concise, as a great way is extremely simple and easy.

The Falun is central to cultivation practice in Falun Buddha Fa. Falun is an intelligent, rotating entity composed of high-energy matter. The Falun that I plant in a practitioner's lower abdomen rotates constantly, twenty-four hours a day. (Genuine practitioners can obtain a Falun by reading my books, watching my lectures on video, listening to my lectures on audiocassette, or studying with Dafa students.) The Falun helps practitioners cultivate automatically. That is, the Falun cultivates practitioners at all times even though they don't perform the exercises at every moment. Of all the cultivation ways introduced to the world today, this is the only one that has achieved "the Fa refining the practitioner."

The rotating Falun possesses the same nature as the universe and is its miniature. The Dharma Wheel of the Buddha School, the *yin-yang* of the Dao School, and everything in the Ten-Directional World[1] are reflected in the Falun. The Falun offers salvation to the practitioner when it rotates inward (clockwise), since it absorbs a great amount of energy from the universe and transforms it into *gong*. The Falun offers salvation to others when rotating outward (counter-clockwise), as it releases energy that can save any being and rectify any abnormal condition; people near the practitioner benefit.

Falun Dafa enables practitioners to assimilate to the supreme nature of the universe, Zhen-Shan-Ren. It differs fundamentally from all other practices and has eight major distinguishing characteristics.

1. Cultivation of a Falun; No Cultivation or Formation of Dan.

The Falun possesses the same nature as the universe and is an intelligent, rotating entity made of high-energy matter. The Falun rotates constantly in the practitioner's lower abdomen and continuously collects energy from the universe, transforming and converting it into *gong*. So practicing cultivation in Falun Dafa can increase practitioners' *gong* and allow them to reach the Unlocking of Gong state unusually quickly. Even those people who have cultivated for over a thousand years have wanted to obtain this Falun but could not. At present, all the practices popular in our society cultivate *dan* and form *dan*. They are called *dan*-method *qigong*. It is very difficult for practitioners of *dan*-method *qigong* practices to achieve the Unlocking of Gong and Enlightenment in this lifetime.

---

[1] Ten-Directional World – the Buddha School conceptualizes the world as consisting of ten directions.

2. The Falun Refines the Practitioner Even When He or She is Not Doing the Exercises.

As practitioners have to work, study, eat, and sleep every day, they are not able to do the exercises twenty-four hours a day. Nonetheless, the Falun rotates constantly, helping practitioners to achieve the effect of doing the exercises twenty-four hours a day. So although practitioners cannot do the exercises every moment, the Falun still refines practitioners without interruption. In short, even though the practitioner might not be doing the exercises, the Fa is refining the practitioner.

Nowhere in the world today has another publicly introduced practice solved the problem of finding time for both work and exercises. Only Falun Dafa has solved this problem. Falun Dafa is the only cultivation way that has achieved "the Fa refining the practitioner."

3. Cultivating the Main Consciousness so that You Obtain Gong.

Falun Dafa cultivates one's Main Consciousness. Practitioners have to consciously cultivate their hearts, abandon all of their attachments, and improve their *xinxing*. You cannot be in a trance or lose yourself when practicing the Great Consummation Way. Your Main Consciousness should govern you at all times as you do the exercises. The *gong* cultivated in this way will grow on your own body and you will obtain *gong* that you yourself can take forth with you. This is why Falun Dafa is so precious—you yourself obtain *gong*.

For thousands of years, all other practices introduced among everyday people have cultivated the practitioner's Assistant Consciousness; the practitioner's flesh body and Main

88

Consciousness have served only as mediums. Upon the practitioner's reaching Consummation, his Assistant Consciousness would ascend and take the *gong* away with it. There is then nothing left for the practitioner's Main Consciousness and his original-body—a lifetime of cultivation effort is in vain. Of course, when a practitioner cultivates his Main Consciousness, his Assistant Consciousness also obtains some *gong* and, naturally, improves along with the Main Consciousness.

4. Cultivation of Both Mind and Body.

"Cultivation of mind" in Falun Dafa refers to the cultivation of one's *xinxing*. Cultivating *xinxing* takes precedence, as it is considered the key to increasing *gong*. In other words, the *gong* that determines one's level is not obtained through doing exercises, but through cultivating one's *xinxing*. One's *gong* level is as high as one's *xinxing* level. The *xinxing* element in Falun Dafa covers a much wider range of things than just virtue; it encompasses many types of things, including virtue.

"Cultivation of body" in Falun Dafa refers to achieving longevity. Through performing the exercises one's original-body undergoes transformation and is preserved. One's Main Consciousness and flesh body merge into one, accomplishing Consummation of the whole. Cultivation of the body fundamentally changes the human body's molecular components. By replacing cells' elements with high-energy matter, the human body is converted into a body made of matter from other dimensions. As a result one will stay young forever. The matter is dealt with at its root. Falun Dafa is thus a genuine cultivation practice of both mind and body.

5. Five Exercises that are Simple and Easy to Learn.

A great way is extremely simple and easy. Viewed broadly, Falun Dafa has a small number of exercise movements, yet the things to be developed are numerous and comprehensive. The movements govern every aspect of the body and the many things that will be developed. All five exercises are completely taught to practitioners. Right from the outset, the areas in the practitioner's body where energy is blocked will be opened, and a great amount of energy will be absorbed from the universe. In a very short period of time the exercises will expel useless substances from the practitioner's body and purify it. The exercises also help practitioners to raise their level, strengthen their divine powers, and arrive at the Pure-White Body state. These five exercises are far beyond the usual exercises that open the meridians or the Great and Small Heavenly Circuits. Falun Dafa provides practitioners with the most convenient and efficient cultivation way, and is also the best and the most precious way.

6. No Use of Mental Activities, No Going Awry, and a Rapid Increase of Gong.

Falun Dafa cultivation practice is free of mind-intent, with no concentration, and is not guided by mind activities. So practicing Falun Dafa is absolutely safe, and it is guaranteed that practitioners will not go awry. The Falun protects practitioners from going awry in the practice as well as from interference by people with poor *xinxing*. Moreover, the Falun can automatically rectify any abnormal condition.

Practitioners begin their cultivation at a very high level. As long as they can bear the toughest hardships of all, endure what is difficult to endure, maintain their *xinxing*, and genuinely practice only one cultivation way, they will be able to reach the state of Three Flowers Gathered Atop the Head within a few years. This is the highest level one can achieve during In-Triple-World-Law cultivation.

7. No Concern for Location, Time, or Direction When Doing the Exercises, and No Concern About Ending the Practice.

The Falun is a miniature of the universe. The universe is rotating, all of its galaxies are rotating, and the Earth is rotating as well. Thus, north, south, east, and west cannot be distinguished. Falun Dafa practitioners practice cultivation according to the fundamental nature of the universe and the law of its evolution. So no matter which direction a practitioner faces, he or she is doing the exercises towards every direction. Since the Falun rotates constantly there is no concept of time; practitioners can do them at any time. The Falun rotates forever and practitioners are unable to stop its rotation, so there is no concept of ending the practice. One finishes one's movements but the practice is not finished.

8. Having the Protection of My Law Bodies, There is No Need to Fear Interference from External Evils.

It is very dangerous for an everyday person to suddenly receive high-level things, as his or her life will instantly be in danger. Practitioners will gain protection from my Law Bodies when they accept my Falun Dafa teachings and genuinely practice cultivation. As long as you persevere in practicing cultivation, my Law Bodies will protect you until you reach Consummation. Should you decide to stop cultivating at some point, my Law Bodies will leave you.

The reason many people do not dare to teach high-level principles is that they are unable to assume the responsibility, and heaven also prohibits their doing so. Falun Dafa is a righteous Fa. One upright mind can subdue all evils, provided that in the practitioner's cultivation practice he maintains his *xinxing*, abandons his attachments, and forgoes any incorrect pursuits, as prescribed by Dafa. Any evil demon will be afraid, and anyone not related to your improvement will not dare to interfere with you or disturb you. The teachings of Falun Dafa are thus completely unlike those of conventional cultivation methods or the *dan*-cultivation theories of other practices and branches of cultivation.

Practicing cultivation in Falun Dafa consists of many levels in both In-Triple-World-Law and Beyond-Triple-World-Law cultivation. This cultivation practice right, at the outset, begins at a very high level. Falun Dafa provides the most convenient cultivation way for its practitioners, as well as for those who have been practicing cultivation for a long time yet have failed to increase their *gong*. When a practitioner's *gong* potency and *xinxing* reach a certain level, he or she can attain an indestructible, never-degenerating body while in the secular world. A practitioner can also achieve the Unlocking of Gong, Enlightenment, and ascension of the whole person to high levels. Those with great determination should study this righteous Fa, strive to achieve the Righteous Attainment, improve their *xinxing,* and abandon their attachments—only then will they be able to reach Consummation.

Chapter V

Illustrations and Explanations
of the Exercise Movements

1. Buddha Showing a Thousand Hands
(*Fo Zhan Qianshou Fa*)[2]

Principles: At the core of Buddha Showing a Thousand Hands is stretching of the body. This stretching unblocks areas where energy is congested, stimulates the energy within the body and under the skin so that it circulates vigorously, and automatically absorbs a great amount of energy from the universe. This enables all of the meridians in a practitioner's body to open at the beginning. When one performs this exercise, the body will have a special feeling of warmth and of the existence of a strong energy field. This is caused by the stretching and opening of all meridians throughout the body. Buddha Showing a Thousand Hands is composed of eight movements. The movements are quite simple, yet they control many things that are evolved by the cultivation method as a whole. At the same time, they enable practitioners to quickly enter the state of being surrounded by an energy field. Practitioners should perform these movements as a foundational exercise. They are usually done first, and are one of the strengthening methods for one's cultivation practice.

---

[2] *Fo Zhan Qianshou Fa* (foah jahn chien-sho fah).

Verse:[3]

身神合一	*Shenshen Heyi*[4]
動靜隨機	*Dongjing Suiji*[5]
頂天獨尊	*Dingtian Duzun*[6]
千手佛立	*Qianshou Foli*[7]

Preparation – Stand naturally with the feet shoulder-width apart. Bend both knees slightly. Keep the knees and hips relaxed. Relax the whole body, but don't become too loose. Tuck the lower jaw in slightly. Touch the tip of the tongue to the hard palate, leave a space between the upper and lower teeth, and close the lips. Gently close the eyes. Maintain a serene expression on the face.

---

[3] The verses are recited once only, in Chinese, right before each exercise. Each exercise has its own specific verse that you may recite out loud or just listen to on the exercise tape.

[4] *Shenshen Heyi* (shuhn-shuhn huh-ee) – Join the Mind and Body Together.

[5] *Dongjing Suiji* (dong-jing sway-jee) – Move or Become Still According to the Energy Mechanisms.

[6] *Dingtian Duzun* (ding-t'yen doo-zun) – As Tall as Heaven and Incomparably Noble.

[7] *Qianshou Foli* (chien-sho foah-lee) – The Thousand-Handed Buddha Stands Upright.

Fig. 1-1

Conjoining the Hands (*Liangshou Jieyin*)[8] – Lift both hands
slightly with the palms facing up. Have the thumb tips lightly
touch each other. Let the other four fingers of each hand meet
and overlap on top of each other. For males, the left hand goes on
top; for females, the right hand goes on top. Have the hands form
an oval shape and hold them at the lower abdominal area. Hold
both upper arms slightly forward with the elbows rounded so
that the underarms are open (Figure 1-1).

---

[8] *Liangshou Jieyin* (liahng-sho jieh-yin) – Conjoin the hands.

Fig. 1-2

Maitreya[9] Stretching His Back (*Mile Shenyao*)[10] – Starting from *Jieyin*,[11] raise both hands upward. When the hands reach the front of the face, separate them and gradually turn the palms upward. When the hands are above the top of the head, have the palms face up. Point the fingers of both hands toward each other (Figure 1-2), with a distance of 20 to 25 cm (*8 to 10 inches*) between them. At the same time, press upward with the heels of both palms, push the head upward, press the feet downward, and stretch the whole body. Stretch for about 2 to 3 seconds, and then

---

[9] *Maitreya* – In Buddhism, Maitreya is the name of the Buddha of the Future, who will come to Earth after Buddha Sakyamuni to offer salvation.

[10] *Mile Shenyao* (mee-luh shuhn-yow)

[11] *Jieyin* (jieh-yin) – short for "Liangshou Jieyin."

96

Fig. 1-3   Fig. 1-4

relax the whole body abruptly. Return the knees and hips to a relaxed position.

Tathagata Pouring Energy into the Top of the Head (*Rulai Guanding*)[12] – Following from the previous movement (Figure 1-3), turn both palms outward at 140° to form a funnel shape. Straighten the wrists and move them downward. As the hands move down, keep the palms facing the chest at a distance of no more than 10 cm (*4 inches*). Continue moving both hands towards the lower abdomen (Figure 1-4).

---

[12] *Rulai Guanding* (roo-lye gwahn-ding)

Fig. 1-5

Pressing the Hands Together in Front of the Chest (*Shuangshou Heshi*)[13] – At the lower abdomen, turn the backs of the hands to face each other, and without pausing, lift the hands up to the chest to form *Heshi* (Figure 1-5). When doing *Heshi,* press both the fingers and the heels of the palms against each other, leaving a hollow space in the center of the palms. Hold the elbows up, with the forearms forming a straight line. (For all of the exercises, keep the hands in the Lotus Palm position[14] except when doing *Heshi* and *Jieyin*).

---

[13] *Shuangshou Heshi* (shwahng-show huh-shr)

[14] *Lotus Palm position* – The hand position to be maintained throughout the exercises. In this position, the palms are open and the fingers are relaxed, but straight. The middle finger of each hand is relaxed so that it bends slightly towards the center of the palm.

Fig. 1-6   Fig. 1-7

Hands Pointing to Heaven and Earth (*Zhangzhi Qiankun*)[15]
– Starting from *Heshi*, separate the hands about 2 to 3 cm (*1 inch*) (Figure 1-6) and turn them in opposite directions. Males, turn the left hand (females, turn the right hand) towards the chest and turn the right hand forward, so that the left hand is on top and the right hand is on the bottom. Both hands should make a straight line with the forearms. Then, extend the left forearm diagonally upward (Figure 1-7). Have its palm facing down and as high as the head. Keep the right hand in front of the chest with the palm

---

[15] *Zhang Zhi Qian Kun* (jahng jrr chien kun) – Note: The description here mainly describes the movements for males. For females, the hand movements are opposite those of males.

99

Fig. 1-8   Fig. 1-9

facing up. After the left arm reaches the proper position, push the head upward, press the feet downward, and stretch the entire body to its limits. Stretch for about 2 to 3 seconds, then immediately relax the entire body. Return the left hand to the front of the chest and form *Heshi* (Figure 1-5). Next, turn the hands in the opposite directions, so that the right hand is on top and the left hand is underneath (Figure 1-8). Extend the right hand and repeat the previous movements of the left hand (Figure 1-9). After stretching, relax the whole body. Move the hands in front of the chest to *Heshi*.

Fig. 1-10

Golden Monkey Splitting its Body (*Jinhou Fenshen*)[16] –
Starting from *Heshi,* extend the arms outward on the sides of the
body, forming a straight line from the shoulders. Push the head
upward, press the feet downward, and straighten the arms on each
side. Stretch outward in four directions, using force throughout
the whole body (Figure 1-10). Stretch for about 2 to 3 seconds.
Immediately relax the entire body and form *Heshi.*

---

[16] *Jinhou Fenshen* (jin-ho fun-shun)

Fig. 1-11

Two Dragons Diving into the Sea (*Shuanglong Xiahai*)[17] –
Starting from *Heshi,* separate the hands and extend them
downward towards the lower front of the body. When the arms
are parallel and straight, the angle between the arms and the body
should be about 30° (Figure 1-11). Push the head upward, press
the feet downward, and stretch the whole body, using force. Stretch
for about 2 to 3 seconds, then immediately relax the entire body.
Move the hands to *Heshi* in front of the chest.

---

[17] *Shuanglong Xiahai* (shwahng-long shiah-high)

Fig. 1-12

Bodhisattva Placing Hands on the Lotus Flower (*Pusa Fulian*)[18] – Starting from *Heshi,* separate both hands while extending them diagonally downward to the sides of the body (Figure 1-12). Straighten the arms so that the angle between the arms and the body is about 30°. At the same time, push the head upward, press the feet downward, and stretch the entire body using force. Stretch for about 2 to 3 seconds, then immediately relax the whole body. Move the hands to *Heshi* in front of the chest.

---

[18] *Pusa Fulian* (poo-sah foo-lien)

Fig. 1-13

Arhat Carrying a Mountain on His Back (*Luohan Beishan*)[19]
– (Figure 1-13) Starting from *Heshi,* separate the hands while
extending them behind the body. At the same time, turn both palms
to face backward. As the hands pass the sides of the body, slowly
bend the wrists upward. When the hands arrive behind the body,
the angle between the wrists and the body should be 45°. At this
point, push the head upward, press the feet downward and stretch
the entire body using force. (Keep the body upright—don't lean
forward, but stretch from the chest.) Stretch for about 2 to 3
seconds, then immediately relax the whole body. Move the hands
to *Heshi* in front of the chest.

---

[19] *Luohan Beishan* (loah-hahn bay-shahn)

104

Fig. 1-14

Vajra[20] Toppling a Mountain (*Jingang Paishan*)[21] –From *Heshi,* separate both hands while pushing forward with the palms. Have the fingers pointing upwards. Keep the hands and shoulders at the same level. Once the arms are extended, push the head upward, press the feet downward, and stretch the whole body using force (Figure 1-14). Stretch for about 2 to 3 seconds, then immediately relax the entire body. Move the hands to *Heshi.*

Overlap the Hands in Front of the Lower Abdomen (*Diekou Xiaofu*)[22] – Starting from *Heshi,* slowly move the hands

---

[20] Vajra – Note: Here, this term refers to a Buddha's warrior attendants.

[21] *Jingang Paishan* (jin-gahng pie-shahn)

[22] *Diekou Xiaofu* (dieh-ko sheeow-foo)

Fig. 1-15   Fig. 1-16

downward, turning the palms towards the abdominal area. When the hands reach the lower abdomen, place one hand in front of the other (Figure 1-15). Males should have the left hand inside; females should have the right hand inside. Have the palm of the outer hand face the back of the inner hand. The distance between the hands, as well as between the inner hand and the lower abdomen, should each be about 3 cm (*1 inch*). Usually one overlaps the hands for 40 to100 seconds.

Closing Position – Conjoin the hands (*Shuangshou Jieyin*) (Figure 1-16).

2. Falun Standing Stance

(*Falun Zhuang Fa*)[23]

Principle: Falun Standing Stance is a tranquil standing meditation composed of four wheel-holding positions. Frequent performance of Falun Standing Stance will facilitate the complete opening of the entire body. It is a comprehensive means of cultivation practice that enhances wisdom, increases strength, raises one's level, and strengthens divine powers. The movements are simple, but much can be achieved through the exercise. Beginners' arms may feel heavy and painful. After doing the exercises, the whole body will immediately feel relaxed, without feeling the kind of fatigue that comes from working. When practitioners increase the time and frequency of the exercise, they can feel a Falun rotating between the arms. The movements of Falun Standing Stance should be done naturally. Don't intentionally pursue swaying. It is normal to move slightly, but obvious swaying should be controlled. The longer the exercise time, the better, but it differs from person to person. Upon entering into tranquility, do not lose awareness that you're exercising, but instead maintain it.

---

[23] *Falun Zhuang Fa* (fah-lun jwahng fah)

Verse:

生慧增力   *Shenghui Zengli*[24]

融心輕體   *Rongxin Qingti*[25]

似妙似悟   *Simiao Siwu*[26]

法輪初起   *Falun Chuqi*[27]

Preparation – Stand naturally with feet shoulder-width apart. Bend both knees slightly. Keep the knees and hips relaxed. Relax the whole body, but don't become too loose. Tuck the lower jaw in slightly. Touch the tip of the tongue to the hard palate, leave a space between the upper and lower teeth, and close the lips. Gently close the eyes. Maintain a serene expression on the face.

Conjoin the hands *(Liangshou Jieyin)* (Figure 2-1)

---

[24] *Shenghui Zengli* (shung-hway zung-lee) – Enhance Wisdom and Strengthen Powers.

[25] *Rongxin Qingti* (rong-shin ching-tee) – Harmonize the Heart and Lighten the Body.

[26] *Simiao Siwu* (szz-meow szz-woo) – As if in a Wondrous and Enlightened State.

[27] *Falun Chuqi* (fah-lun choo-chee) – Falun Begins to Rise.

Fig. 2-1   Fig. 2-2

Holding the Wheel in Front of the Head (*Touqian Baolun*)[28] –
Start from *Jieyin* (the conjoined hand position). Slowly raise both
hands from the abdomen, separating them in the process. When
the hands are in front of the head, the palms should face the face
at eyebrow level (Figure 2-2). Have the fingers of the hands
pointing toward one another, with a distance of 15 cm (*6 inches*)
between them. Form a circle with the arms. Relax the whole body.

---

[28] *Touqian Baolun* (toe-chien bao-lun)

Fig. 2-3   Fig. 2-4

Holding the Wheel in Front of the Lower Abdomen (*Fuqian Baolun*)[29] – Slowly move both hands downward. Keep the arms in the wheel-holding position as they reach the lower abdominal area (Figure 2-3). Hold both elbows forward, keeping the underarms open. Keep the palms facing upward, the fingers pointing toward one another, and the arms in the shape of a circle.

Holding the Wheel Above the Head (*Touding Baolun*)[30] – While maintaining the wheel-holding position, slowly raise the hands until they are over the head (Figure 2-4). Have the fingers

---

[29] *Fuqian Baolun* (foo-chien bao-lun)

[30] *Touding Baolun* (toe-ding bao-lun)

Fig. 2-5

of both hands pointing toward one another, and the palms facing downward. Keep a distance of 20 to 30 cm (*8 to 12 inches*) between the fingertips of both hands. Have the arms form a circle. Keep the shoulders, arms, elbows, and wrists relaxed.

Holding the Wheel on Both Sides of the Head (*Liangce Baolun*)[31] – Starting from the previous position, move both hands downward next to the sides of the head (Figure 2-5). Keep the palms facing the ears, with both shoulders relaxed and the forearms upright. Don't keep the hands too close to the ears.

---

[31] *Liangce Baolun* (liang-tsuh bao-lun)

Fig. 2-6   Fig. 2-7

Overlap the Hands in Front of the Lower Abdomen (*Diekou Xiaofu*) (Figure 2-6) – Move the hands downward to the lower abdomen. Overlap the hands.

Closing Position – *Liangshou Jieyin* (Conjoin the hands) (Figure 2-7).

3. Penetrating the Two Cosmic Extremes
(*Guantong Liangji Fa*)[32]

Principle: Penetrating the Two Cosmic Extremes channels the cosmos' energy and mixes it with the energy inside one's body. A great amount of energy is expelled and taken in during this exercise, enabling a practitioner to purify his or her body in a very short time. At the same time, the exercise opens the meridians on top of the head and unblocks the passages underneath the feet. The hands move up and down according to the energy inside the body and the mechanisms outside the body. The upward-moving energy dashes out of the top of the head and travels directly to the upper cosmic extreme; the downward-moving energy is ejected out from the bottom of the feet and rushes directly to the lower cosmic extreme. After the energy returns from both extremes it is then emitted in the opposite direction. The hand movements are done nine times.

After the one-handed gliding up and down movements are done nine times, both hands are to glide up and down nine times. Then, the Falun is turned clockwise four times in front of the lower abdomen in order to spin the outside energy into the body. The movements end by conjoining the hands.

Before doing the exercise, imagine you are two empty barrels, standing upright between heaven and earth, gigantic and incomparably tall. This helps channel the energy.

---

[32] *Guantong Liangji Fa* (gwahn-tong liang-jee fah)

Verse:

淨化本體	*Jinghua Benti*[33]
法開頂底	*Fakai Dingdi*[34]
心慈意猛	*Xinci Yimeng*[35]
通天澈地	*Tongtian Chedi*[36]

Preparation – Stand naturally with feet shoulder-width apart. Bend both knees slightly. Keep the knees and hips relaxed. Relax the whole body, but don't become too loose. Tuck the lower jaw in slightly. Touch the tip of the tongue to the hard palate, leave a space between the upper and lower teeth, and close the lips. Gently close the eyes. Maintain a serene expression on the face.

---

[33] *Jinghua Benti* (jing-hwa bun-tee) – Purify the Body.

[34] *Fakai Dingdi* (fah-kye ding-dee) – The Fa Unlocks the Top and Bottom Energy Passages.

[35] *Xinci Yimeng* (shin-tszz ee-mung) – The Heart is Benevolent and the Will is Strong.

[36] *Tongtian Chedi* (tong-t'yen chuh-dee) – Reach the Zenith of Heaven and the Nadir of Earth.

114

Fig. 3-1   Fig. 3-2

Conjoin the Hands (*Liangshou Jieyin*) – (Figure 3-1)

Press the Hands Together in Front of the Chest (*Shuangshou Heshi*) – (Figure 3-2)

Fig. 3-3   Fig. 3-4

One-Handed Gliding Up-and-Down Movement (*Danshou Chong'guan*)[37] – From *Heshi*, simultaneously glide one hand upward and the other hand downward. The hands should glide slowly along with the energy mechanisms outside the body. The energy inside the body moves up and down simultaneously with the hand movements (Figure 3-3). Males start by gliding the left hand upward; females start by gliding the right hand upward. Pass that hand in front of the face and extend it above the head. Meanwhile, slowly lower the right hand (females, the left hand). Then switch the positions of the hands (Figure 3-4). Keep the palms facing the body at a distance of no more than 10 cm (*4 inches*). Keep the entire body relaxed. One up-and-down movement of each hand is one count. Repeatedly glide the hands up and down for nine counts.

---

[37] *Danshou Chong'guan* (dahn-show chong-gwan)

116

Fig. 3-5   Fig. 3-6

Two-Handed Gliding Up-and-Down Movement (*Shuangshou Chong'guan*)[38] – After the one-handed gliding up and down movement, keep the left hand (right hand for females) up and waiting, and slowly bring the other hand up so that both hands are pointing upward (Figure 3-5). Then slowly glide both hands downward at the same time (Figure 3-6).

When gliding both hands up and down, keep the palms facing the body at a distance of no more than 10 cm (*4 inches*). A complete up-and-down movement is one count. Repeatedly glide the hands up and down for nine counts.

---

[38] *Shuangshou Chong'guan* (shwahng-show chong-gwan)

117

Fig. 3-7   Fig. 3-8

Turning the Falun With Two Hands (*Shuangshou Tuidong Falun*)[39] – After the ninth two-handed gliding up and down movement, move both hands downward past the head and over the chest until they reach the lower abdominal area (Figure 3-7). Turn the Falun with both hands (Figure 3-8, Figure 3-9). The left hand goes inside for males, and the right hand goes inside for females. Keep a distance of about 2-3 cm (*1 inch*) between the hands and also between the inner hand and the lower abdomen.

---

[39] *Shuangshou Tuidong Falun* (shwahng-show tway-dong fah-lun)

118

Fig. 3-9   Fig. 3-10

Turn the Falun clockwise 4 times to spin the energy from the outside to the inside of the body. While turning the Falun, keep the hands within the area of the lower abdomen.

Closing Position – *Liangshou Jieyin* (Conjoin the hands) (Figure 3-10).

4. Falun Heavenly Circuit

(*Falun Zhoutian Fa*)[40]

Principle: Falun Heavenly Circuit enables the energy of the human body to circulate over large areas—that is, not just in one or several meridians, but from the entire *yin* side to the entire *yang* side of the body, back and forth continuously. This exercise is far beyond the usual methods of opening the meridians or the Great and Small Heavenly Circuits. Falun Heavenly Circuit is an intermediate-level cultivation method. With the previous three exercises as a base, the meridians of the entire body (including the Great Heavenly Circuit) can be quickly opened through performing this exercise. From top to bottom, the meridians will be gradually connected throughout the entire body. The most outstanding feature of this exercise is its use of the Falun rotation to rectify all abnormal conditions in the human body. This enables the human body—a small universe—to return to its original state and enables all meridians inside the body to be unblocked. When this state is reached, one has achieved a very high level within In-Triple-World-Law cultivation. When doing this exercise, both hands follow the energy mechanisms. The movements are gradual, slow, and smooth.

---

[40] *Falun Zhoutian Fa* (fah-lun jo-tien fah)

Verse:

旋法至虚   *Xuanfa Zhixu*[41]

心清似玉   *Xinqing Siyu*[42]

返本歸真   *Fanben Guizhen*[43]

悠悠似起   *Youyou Siqi*[44]

Preparation – Stand naturally with feet shoulder-width apart. Bend both knees slightly. Keep the knees and hips relaxed. Relax the whole body, but don't become too loose. Tuck the lower jaw in slightly. Touch the tip of the tongue to the hard palate, leave a space between the upper and lower teeth, and close the lips. Gently close the eyes. Maintain a serene expression on the face.

---

[41] *Xuanfa Zhixu* (shwen-fah jhr-sheeu) – The Revolving Fa Reaches the Void.

[42] *Xinqing Siyu* (shin-ching szz-yoo) – The Heart is Clear Like Pure Jade.

[43] *Fanben Guizhen* (fahn-bun gway-juhn) – Returning to Your Origin and True Self.

[44] *Youyou Siqi* (yo-yo szz-chee) – You Feel Light, as if Floating.

121

Fig. 4-1   Fig. 4-2

Conjoin the Hands (*Liangshou Jieyin*) – (Figure 4-1)

Press the Hands Together in Front of the Chest (*Shuangshou Heshi*) – (Figure 4-2)

Fig. 4-3   Fig. 4-4

Separate the hands from *Heshi*. Move them downward to the lower abdomen while turning both palms to face the body. Keep a distance of no more than 10 cm (*4 inches*) between the hands and the body. After passing the lower abdomen, extend the hands downward between the legs. Move the hands downward with palms facing the inner sides of the legs and, at the same time, bend at the waist and squat down (Figure 4-3). When the fingertips get close to the ground, move the hands in a circle from the front of the feet, along the outside of the feet to the heels (Figure 4-4).

Fig. 4-5   Fig. 4-6

Bend both wrists slightly and raise the hands along the back of
the legs (Figure 4-5). Straighten the waist while lifting the hands
up along the back (Figure 4-6).

Chapter VI

Mechanics and Principles
of the Exercise Movements

1. The First Exercise

The first exercise is called Buddha Showing a Thousand Hands. Just as the name suggests, it's as if a thousand-handed Buddha or a thousand-handed Bodhisattva is displaying his or her hands. Of course, it is impossible for us to do a thousand movements—you wouldn't be able to remember all of them, and performing them would wear you out. We use eight simple, basic movements in this exercise to represent that idea. Though simple, these eight movements enable the hundreds of meridians in our bodies to open. Let me tell you why we say that from the outset our practice begins at a very high level. It's because we don't open just one or two meridians, the Ren and Du meridians, or the eight Extra Meridians. Instead, we open all of the meridians, and each of them is in simultaneous motion from the very beginning. We thus start practicing at a very high level right from the outset.

One has to stretch and relax the body when doing this exercise. The hands and legs need to be well coordinated. Through stretching and relaxing, the areas of congested energy in the body are unblocked. Of course, the movements would have no effect whatsoever if I didn't plant a set of mechanisms in your body. When stretching, the whole body is stretched gradually to its limit—even to the extent that you feel as though you are splitting into two people. The body stretches as if it becomes very tall and large. No mind-intent is used. After stretching out to the limit,

141

the body is to relax abruptly—you should relax right away once you stretch to the limit. The effect of such movement is like that with a leather bag filled with air: when squeezed, its air gushes out; when one lifts one's hand off the bag, the air is drawn back in and new energy is taken in. With this mechanism at work, the blocked areas of the body are opened.

When the body is stretching, the heels are pressed down firmly and strength is used to push the head up. It's as if all the meridians in your body are being stretched until open and then relaxed abruptly—you should relax abruptly after stretching. Your whole body is immediately opened through this type of motion. Of course, we also have to plant various mechanisms in your body. When the arms are stretching, they're stretched gradually and forcefully until the limit is reached. The Dao School teaches how to move energy along the three *yin* and three *yang* meridians. In fact, there are not only the three *yin* and three *yang* meridians, but also hundreds of crisscrossing meridians in the arms. They all have to be stretched open and unblocked. We open all the meridians right at the outset of our practice. Of the ordinary cultivation practices, the genuine ones—this then excludes those that harness *qi*—use the method of bringing hundreds of meridians into motion via one energy channel. It takes these practices a long time—countless years—to open all of the meridians. Our practice aims directly at opening all meridians at the outset, and, therefore, we begin by practicing at a very high level. Everyone should grasp this key point.

Next, I will talk about the standing posture. You need to stand naturally with the feet shoulder-width apart. The feet don't have to be parallel, as we do not have things from the martial arts here. Many exercise practices' standing stances originated from the Horse Stance of the martial arts. Since the Buddha School teaches the offering of salvation to all beings, your feet shouldn't always be turned inward. The knees and hips are relaxed, bending the knees slightly. When the knees are bent slightly, the meridians there are open; when one stands straight up, the meridians there are rigid and blocked. The body is kept upright and relaxed. You need to completely relax from the inside out, but without becoming too loose. The head should remain upright.

The eyes are closed when performing these five exercises. But when learning the movements, you have to keep the eyes open and watch to see if your movements are correct. Later on, once you have learned the movements and are performing them on your own, the exercises ought to be done with eyes closed. The tip of the tongue touches the hard palate, a space is maintained between the upper and lower teeth, and the lips are closed. Why does the tongue need to touch the hard palate? As you may know, during genuine practice it's not only the superficial skin-deep heavenly circuit that's in motion, but also every meridian in the body that intersects vertically or horizontally. Besides there being superficial meridians, there are also meridians on the internal organs and in the gaps between the internal organs. The mouth is empty, so it relies on the raised tongue to form a bridge inside that strengthens the energy flow during the meridians' circulation and allows the energy to form a circuit through the tongue. The closed lips serve as an external bridge that allows surface energy to circulate. Why do we leave a space between the upper and lower teeth? It's because if your teeth are clenched during the exercise, the energy will make them clench tighter and tighter during its circulation. Whichever part of the body is tense can't be fully transformed. So any part that's not relaxed will end up being excluded and not transformed or evolved. The upper and lower teeth will relax if you leave a space between them. These are the basic requirements for the exercise movements. There are three transitional movements that will later be repeated in other exercises. I would now like to explain them here.

Liangshou Heshi (Pressing Both Hands Together in Front of the Chest). When doing *Heshi,* the forearms form a straight line and the elbows are suspended so that the underarms are hollow. If the underarms are pressed tight, the energy channels will be completely blocked there. The fingertips are not raised as high as the front of the face, but just to the front of the chest. They are not to be leaned against the body. A hollow space is kept between the palms, and the heels of the palms should be pressed together as much as possible. Everyone needs to remember this position, as it's repeated many times.

Diekou Xiaofu (Overlapping the Hands in Front of the Lower Abdomen). The elbows should be suspended. During the exercises you have to hold the elbows out. We emphasize this with good reason: If the underarms are not open, energy will be blocked and unable to flow through. When doing this position, the left hand is inside for males; the right hand is inside for females. The hands must not touch each other—a palm's width is kept between them. A two-palms' width is kept between the inner hand and the body, without allowing the hand to touch the body. Why is this? As we know, there are many internal and external channels. In our practice we rely on the Falun to open them, especially the Laogong[58] point on one's hands. In fact, the Laogong point is a field that exists not only in our flesh body, but also in all of our bodies' forms of existence in other dimensions. Its field is very large, and even exceeds the surface of the flesh body's hands. All of its fields have to be opened, so we rely on the Falun to do this. The hands are kept apart because there are Falun rotating on them—on both hands. When the hands overlap in front of the lower abdomen at the end of the exercises, the energy carried on them is very strong. Another purpose of *Diekou Xiaofu* is to

---

[58] Laogong (laow-gong) – the acupuncture point at the center of one's palm.

144

strengthen both the Falun in the lower abdomen and the field of *dantian*. There are many things—more than ten thousand of them—that will be evolved from this field.

There's another position called *Jie Dingyin*.[59] We call it *Jieyin* (Conjoining the Hands) for short. Take a look at the conjoined hands: it's not to be done casually. The thumbs are raised, forming an oval shape. The fingers are joined together lightly with the fingers of the lower hand positioned against the gaps between the fingers of the upper hand. This is how it should be. When conjoining the hands, the left hand is on top for males, while the right hand is on top for females. Why is this? It's because the male body is one of pure *yang* and the female body is one of pure *yin*. In order to attain a balance of *yin* and *yang*, males should suppress the *yang* and give play to the *yin*, while females should suppress the *yin* and give play to the *yang*. So some of the movements are different for males and females. When conjoining the hands, the elbows are suspended—they need to be held out. As you may know, the center of *dantian* is two finger-widths below the navel. This is also the center of our Falun. So the conjoined hands are to be placed a bit lower down to hold the Falun. When relaxing the body, some people relax their hands but not their legs. The legs and hands have to be coordinated to simultaneously relax and stretch.

2. The Second Exercise

The second exercise is called Falun Standing Stance. Its movements are quite simple, as there are only four wheel-holding positions—they are very easy to learn. Nonetheless, this is a challenging and demanding exercise. How is it demanding? All

---

[59] *Jie Dingyin* (jieh ding-yin) – Conjoining Both Hands.

standing-stance exercises require standing still for a long time. One's arms will feel painful when the hands are held up for a long time. So this exercise is demanding. The posture for Standing Stance is the same as that of the first exercise, but there's no stretching and one simply stands with the body relaxed. All of the four basic positions involve wheel holding. Simple as they are—only four basic positions—this is Dafa cultivation, so it couldn't be that each single movement is merely for cultivating one particular supernormal ability or one minor thing; each single movement involves many things. It wouldn't do if each and every thing required one movement to evolve it. I can tell you that the things I installed in your lower abdomen and the things evolved in our cultivation way number in the hundreds of thousands. If you had to use one movement to cultivate each one of them, just imagine: hundreds of thousands of movements would be involved, and you wouldn't be able to finish doing them in a day. You would exhaust yourself and still might not be able to remember them all.

There's a saying, "A great way is extremely simple and easy." The exercises control the transformation of all things as a whole. So it would be even better if there were no movement at all when doing tranquil cultivation exercises. Simple movements can also control on a large scale the simultaneous transformation of many things. The simpler the movements, the more complete the transformation is likely to be, as they control everything on a large scale. There are four wheel-holding positions in this exercise. When you are holding the wheels you will feel the rotation of a large Falun between your arms. Almost every practitioner is able to feel it. When doing Falun Standing Stance, no one is allowed to sway or jump as with the practices where possessing spirits are in control. Swaying and jumping are no good—that's not practicing. Have you ever seen a Buddha, Dao, or God jumping or swaying like that? None of them do that.

3. The Third Exercise

The third exercise is called Penetrating the Two Cosmic Extremes. This exercise is also quite simple. As its name suggests, this exercise is for sending energy to the two "cosmic extremes." How far are the two extremes of this boundless cosmos? This is beyond your imagination, so the exercise doesn't involve mind-intent. We perform the exercises by following the mechanisms. Thus, your hands move along with the mechanisms that I've installed in your body. The first exercise also has these kinds of mechanisms. I didn't mention this to you on the first day because you shouldn't go seeking this sensation before becoming familiar with the movements. I was concerned that you wouldn't be able to remember all of them. You will actually find that when you stretch and relax your arms they automatically return, by themselves. This is caused by the mechanisms installed in your body, something known in the Dao School as the Hand-Gliding Mechanisms. After finishing one movement, you will notice that your hands automatically glide out to do the next one. This sensation will gradually become more obvious as your exercise time lengthens. All of these mechanisms will revolve on their own after I've given them to you. In fact, when you're not doing the exercises, the *gong* is cultivating you under the function of the Falun's mechanism. The subsequent exercises also have mechanisms. The posture for this exercise is the same as that of Falun Standing Stance. There's no stretching, as one merely stands with the body relaxed. There are two kinds of hand movements. One is a one-handed gliding up and down movement, that is, one hand glides up while the other hand glides down—the hands switch positions. One up-and-down movement of each hand is counted as one time, and the movement is repeated for a total of nine times. After eight and a half times are performed, the lower hand is lifted, and the two-handed gliding up and down movement begins. It is also done nine times. Later on, should you wish to do more repetitions and increase the amount of exercise, you can perform it eighteen times—the number has to be a multiple of nine. This is because the mechanism will alter after the ninth time; it has been fixed at the ninth time. You can't always count when doing the exercises in the future. When the mechanisms become very strong, they will end the movements on their own on the ninth time. Your hands will be drawn together, since the mechanisms change automatically. You won't even have to count the number of times, as it's guaranteed that your hands will be led to turn the Falun upon finishing the ninth gliding movement. In the future you shouldn't always count, as you need to perform the exercises in an intention-free state. Having intention is an attachment. No mind-intent is used in high-level cultivation practice—it's completely in a state free of intention. Of course, there are people who say that doing movements is itself full of intention. This is an incorrect understanding. If the movements are said to be full of intention, then what about the hand signs made by Buddhas, or the conjoined hands and meditation done by Zen Buddhist monks and monks in temples? Does the argument for their "having intention" refer to how many movements and hand signs are involved? Does the number of movements determine if one is in a state free of intention or not? Are there attachments if there are more movements and no attachments if there are fewer movements? It's not the movements that count, but rather, it's whether one's mind has attachments and whether there are things one can't let go of. It's the mind that matters. We perform the exercises by following the mechanisms and gradually abandoning our intention-driven thinking, reaching a state free of mind-intent.

148

Our bodies undergo a special kind of transformation during the upward and downward gliding of the hands. Meanwhile, the channels atop our heads will be opened, something known as "Opening the Top of the Head." The passages at the bottoms of our feet will also be unblocked. These passages are more than just the Yongquan[60] point, which is itself actually a field. Because the human body has different forms of existence in other dimensions, your bodies will progressively expand as you practice and the volume of your *gong* will become larger and larger such that [your body in other dimensions] will exceed the size of your human body.

While one is doing the exercises, the Opening of the Top of the Head will occur at the head's crown. This Opening the Top of the Head that we refer to isn't the same as that in Tantrism. In Tantrism it refers to opening one's Baihui point and then inserting a piece of "lucky straw" into it. It's a cultivation technique taught in Tantrism. Our Opening the Top of the Head is different. Ours refers to communication between the universe and our brain. It's known that general Buddhist cultivation also has Opening the Top of the Head, but it's seldom revealed. In some cultivation practices it's considered an achievement if a fissure is opened at the top of one's head. Actually, they still have a long way to go. What extent should genuine Opening the Top of the Head reach? One's crania have to be opened completely and then forever in a state of automatic opening-and-closing. One's brain will be in constant communication with the vast universe. Such a state will exist, and this is genuine Opening the Top of the Head. Of course, this doesn't refer to the cranium in this dimension—that would prove too frightening. It's the crania in other dimensions.

---

[60] Yongquan (yong-chew-en) – the acupuncture point at the center of the sole of one's foot.

This exercise is also very easy to perform. The required standing posture is the same as with the previous two exercises, though there's no stretching as with the first exercise. Neither is stretching required in the exercises that follow. One just needs to stand in a relaxed way and keep the posture unchanged. While performing the up and down hand gliding, everyone has to ensure that his or her hands follow the mechanisms. Your hands actually glide along with the mechanisms in the first exercise as well. Your hands will automatically glide to *Heshi* when you finish stretching and relaxing your body. These kinds of mechanisms have been installed in your body. We perform the exercises along with the mechanisms so that these may be reinforced. There's no need for you to cultivate *gong* by yourself, for the mechanisms assume that role. You just perform the exercises to reinforce the mechanisms. You will sense their existence once you grasp this essential point and perform the movements correctly. The distance between your hands and your body is no more than 10 centimeters (*4 inches*). Your hands need to stay within this range to feel the mechanisms' existence. Some people can never sense the mechanisms since they don't relax completely. They will slowly come to sense them after doing the exercise for a while. During the exercise one should not use intention to draw *qi* upward, and neither should one think of pouring *qi* or pressing *qi* inward. The hands should face the body at all times. There's one thing that I wish to point out: Some people move their hands close to their body, but the moment their hands are in front of their face they slide their hands away for fear of touching the face. Things won't work if the hands are too far away from the face. Your hands have to glide upward and downward close to your face and body, as long as they don't get so close that they touch your clothes. Everyone has to follow this important point. If your movements are correct, your palm will always face inward when your hand is in the upward position during the one-handed up-and-down gliding movement.

Don't just pay attention to the upper hand when doing the one-handed up-and-down gliding movement. The lower hand also has to reach its position since the upward and downward movements occur simultaneously. The hands glide up and down at the same time and reach their positions at the same time. The hands are not to overlap when moving along the chest, or the mechanisms will be damaged. The hands are to be kept separate, having each hand cover only one side of the body. The arms are straightened, but this does not mean they're not relaxed. Both the arms and the body should be relaxed, but the arms need to be straightened. Because the hands move along with the mechanisms, you will feel that there are mechanisms and a force leading your fingers to glide upward. When doing the two-handed up-and-down gliding movement, the arms may open a little bit, but they should not be spaced too far apart since the energy moves upward. Pay special attention to this when doing the two-handed up-and-down gliding movement. Some people are accustomed to supposedly, "holding *qi* and pouring it into the top of the head." They always move their hands downward with the palms facing down and lift their hands upward with the palms facing up. That's no good—the palms must face the body. Although the movements are called upward and downward gliding, they are actually done by the mechanisms given to you—it's the mechanisms that assume this function. There is no mind-intent involved. None of the five exercises use any mind-intent. There's one thing about the third exercise: Before doing the exercise, you imagine that you are an empty barrel or two empty barrels. It is to give you the idea that the energy will flow smoothly. That's the main purpose. The hands are in the lotus palm position.

Now I'm going to talk about turning the Falun with your hands. How do you turn it? Why should we turn the Falun? The energy released by our exercises travels inconceivably far, reaching the two cosmic extremes, but there is no mind-intent used. This is unlike ordinary practices, in which what's known as "collecting *yang qi* from heaven and *yin qi* from earth" is still limited to within Earth's boundary. Our exercise enables energy to penetrate the Earth and to reach the cosmic extremes. Your mind is incapable of imagining how vast and distant the cosmic extremes are—it's simply inconceivable. Even if you were given a whole day to imagine it, you still wouldn't be able to grasp how large it is or where the boundary of the universe is. Even if you thought with your mind completely unrestrained, you still wouldn't be able to know the answer by the time you had become exhausted. Genuine cultivation practice is done in a state free of intention, so there's no need for any mind-intent. You don't need to be concerned with much in order to perform the exercises— just follow the mechanisms. My mechanisms will assume this function. Please note that since energy is emitted very far during the exercise, we have to turn our Falun manually at the end of the exercise to give them a push and return the energy instantly. Turning the Falun four times suffices. If you turn it more than four times your stomach will feel distended. The Falun is turned clockwise. The hands shouldn't move beyond the body when turning the Falun, as that would be turning it too widely. The point two finger-widths below the navel should be used as the center of the axis. The elbows are raised and suspended, and both the hands and forearms are kept straight. It's necessary to do the movements correctly when you first start to do the exercises, or the mechanisms will become distorted.

4. The Fourth Exercise

The fourth exercise is called Falun Heavenly Circuit. Here we've used two terms from the Buddha School and the Dao School[61] so that everyone understands it. This exercise used to be called Turning the Great Falun. This exercise slightly resembles the Dao School's Great Heavenly Circuit, but our requirements are different. All of the meridians should have been opened during the first exercise, so while doing the fourth exercise all of them will simultaneously be in motion. Meridians exist on the surface of the human body as well as in its depths, in each of its layers, and in the spaces between its interior organs. So how does the energy travel in our practice? We require all meridians of the human body to attain simultaneous motion, rather than having just one or two meridians circulating or the eight Extra Meridians revolving. The energy flow is thus quite powerful. If the front and the back of the human body are indeed divided into a *yang* and *yin* side, respectively, then the energy of each side is moving; that is, the energy of the entire side is in motion. As long as you're going to practice Falun Dafa, from now on you have to let go of any mind-intent you have used for guiding the heavenly circuit since in our practice all the meridians are opened and put into simultaneous motion. The movements are quite simple and the standing posture is the same as that of the previous exercise, except for your having to bend at the waist somewhat. Your movements should follow the mechanisms here as well. These kinds of mechanisms also exist in each of the previous exercises, and the movements need to again follow the mechanisms. The mechanisms that I install outside of your body for this particular exercise aren't common ones but a layer of mechanisms that can bring all of the meridians into motion. They will drive all of your

---

[61] Respectively, "Falun" and "Heavenly Circuit."

body's meridians into continuous rotation—rotation that continues even when you're not doing the exercises. They will also rotate in reverse at the appropriate time. The mechanisms rotate in both directions; there is no need for you to work for those things. You should simply follow what we've taught you and should be free of any mind-intent. It's this layer of large meridians that lead you to finish the exercise.

The energy of the entire body has to be in motion when doing Heavenly Circuit. In other words, if the human body is indeed divided into a *yin* and a *yang* side, then the energy circulates from the *yang* side to the *yin* side, from the body's interior to its exterior, back and forth, while hundreds or thousands of meridians circulate simultaneously. Those of you who used to perform other heavenly circuits and used different kinds of mind-intent or had different kinds of ideas about the heavenly circuit have to let go of all of them when practicing our Dafa. Those things you practiced were too small. It's simply ineffective to have just one or two meridians in motion, as progress will be too slow. From observing the surface of the human body it's known that there exist meridians. The meridians actually intersect vertically and horizontally inside the body, just like blood vessels, and their density is even higher than that of blood vessels. They exist in the layers of the human body in different dimensions, that is, from the surface of your body to the bodies in deep dimensions, including in the spaces between the interior organs. If the human body is indeed divided into two sides, one *yin* and one *yang*, it must be that the whole side, either the front or the back, circulates at the same time when you perform the exercises—it is no longer one or two meridians. Those of you who used to do other heavenly circuits will ruin your practice if you perform our exercise using any mind-intent. So you must not cling to any of the mind-intent you used to use. Even if your previous heavenly circuit was opened, that still means nothing. We've already far exceeded that, as all the meridians of our practice are set in motion from the outset. The standing posture is no different from those in the previous exercises, with the exception of some bending at the waist. During the exercises, we require the hands to follow the mechanisms. It's just like the third exercise, in which the hands float up and down with the mechanisms. One should follow the mechanisms during the entire circuit when performing this exercise.

The movements of this exercise need to be repeated nine times. If you'd like to do them more you can do them eighteen times, but you have to be sure that the number is a multiple of nine. Later on when you reach a certain level it won't be necessary to count the number of times. Why is that? It's because repeated performance of the movements for nine times will make the mechanisms become fixed. After the ninth time, the mechanisms will make your hands naturally overlap in front of the lower abdomen. After you've been doing the exercise for some time, these mechanisms will automatically lead the hands to overlap in front of the lower abdomen after the ninth time, and you will no longer need to count. Of course, when you have just begun to do the exercises, the number of times still has to be counted, since the mechanisms aren't strong enough.

5. The Fifth Exercise

The fifth exercise is called Strengthening Divine Powers. It's something of high-level cultivation practice that I used to do by myself. I'm now making it public without any modifications. Because I no longer have time... it will be very difficult for me to have another opportunity to teach you in person. I now teach you everything at once so that later on you will have a way to practice at high levels. The movements of this exercise are not complex, either, as a great way is extremely simple and easy—complicated movements are not necessarily good. Yet this exercise controls the transformation of many things on a large scale. It's a very challenging and demanding exercise, as you need to sit in meditation for a long time to complete this exercise. This exercise is independent, so one doesn't need to perform the previous four exercises before doing this one. Of course, all of our exercises are very flexible. If you don't have much time today and can only do the first exercise, then you may just do the first one. You may even perform the exercises in a different order. Say your schedule is tight today and you just want to do the second exercise, the third exercise, or the fourth exercise—that, too, is all right. If you have more time, you can do more; if you have less time, you can do less—the exercises are quite convenient. When you perform them you are reinforcing the mechanisms that I've installed in you and are strengthening your Falun and *dantian*.

Our fifth exercise is independent and consists of three parts. The first part is performing the hand signs, which are for adjusting your body. The movements are quite simple and there are just a few of them. The second part strengthens your divine powers. There are several fixed positions that deliver your supernormal abilities and divine powers from the inside of your body to your hands for strengthening during the exercise. That's why the fifth exercise is called Strengthening Divine Powers—it reinforces one's supernormal abilities. The next part is sitting in meditation and entering into *ding*. The exercise is comprised of these three parts.

I'll first talk about the seated meditation. There are two kinds of leg crossing for meditation; in genuine practice there are just two ways to fold one's legs. Some people claim that there are more than two ways: "Just take a look at Tantrism's practice—aren't there many ways to fold one's legs?" Let me tell you that those are not leg-crossing methods but exercise positions and movements. There are only two kinds of genuine leg crossing: one is called "single-leg crossing" and the other is called "double-leg crossing."

Let me explain the single-leg crossing position. This position can only be used as a transition, as a last resort, when you aren't able to sit with both legs crossed. Single-leg crossing is done with one leg below and the other above. While sitting in the single-leg crossing position, many people hurt in their anklebones and are unable to bear the pain for long. Even before their legs have begun hurting, the pain caused by their anklebones has already become unbearable. The anklebones will shift backwards if you can turn your feet over so that their soles face upward. Of course, even though I've told you to do the exercise this way, you might be unable to achieve this at the very beginning. You can work on it gradually.

There are many different theories about the single-leg crossing. Practices in the Dao School teach "drawing in without releasing out," which means that energy is always being drawn in and never released out. The Daoists try to avoid dispersing their energy. So how do they achieve that? They are particular about sealing off their acupuncture points. Often when they cross their legs they close off the Yongquan point of one foot by putting it underneath the other leg and tuck the Yongquan point of the other foot under the upper part of the opposite thigh. It's the same with their *Jieyin* position. They use one thumb to press the opposite hand's Laogong point, and use the other hand's Laogong point to cover the opposite hand while both hands cover the lower abdomen.

The leg crossing in our Dafa doesn't have any of those requirements. All of the cultivation practices in the Buddha School—regardless of which cultivation path—teach the offering of salvation to all beings. So they're not afraid of giving off energy. As a matter of fact, even if your energy is released and consumed, you can later make it up in the course of your practice without losing anything. That is because your *xinxing* will have reached a certain level—your energy won't be lost. But you have to endure hardships if you want to raise your level further. In that case your energy won't be lost whatsoever. We don't ask much for the single-leg crossing since we actually require double-leg crossing, not single-leg crossing. Since there are people who can't cross both legs yet, I will take this opportunity to speak a little bit about the single-leg crossing position. You may do the single-leg crossing if you can't yet sit with both legs crossed, but you still need to work to gradually put both of your legs up. Our single-leg crossing position requires of males that the right leg be below and the left leg above; for females, the left leg is to be below and the right leg above. In fact, genuine single-leg crossing is very difficult since it requires the crossed legs to form one line; I don't think that doing a one-line leg crossing is any easier than doing the double-leg crossing. The lower part of the legs should be basically parallel—this has to be achieved—and there should be space between the legs and the pelvis. Single-leg crossing is hard to do. These are the general requirements for the single-leg crossing position, but we don't ask this of people. Why is that? It's because this exercise demands that one sit with both legs crossed.

I'll explain double-leg crossing now. We require you to sit with both legs crossed, which means that from the single-leg crossing position you pull the leg from underneath to the top, pull it from the outside, not the inside. This is double-leg crossing. Some people do a relatively tight leg crossing. By doing so, the

158

soles of both feet face up and they can achieve Five Centers Facing Heaven. This is how the genuine Five Centers Facing Heaven is done in Buddha School exercises in general—the top of the head, the two palms, and the soles of both feet face upward. If you want to do a loose leg crossing, it's all right to do it however you like; some people prefer a loose leg crossing. But all we require is sitting with both legs crossed—a loose leg crossing is fine, just as is a tight one.

The tranquil meditation requires sitting in meditation for a long time. During the meditation there should be no mental activity—don't think about anything. We've said that your Main Consciousness has to be aware, for this practice cultivates you yourself. You should progress with an alert mind. How do we perform the meditation? We require that each of you must know that you are doing the exercise there, no matter how deeply you meditate. You absolutely should not enter into a state in which you're aware of nothing. So what particular state will occur? As you sit there you will feel wonderful and very comfortable, as if you were sitting inside an eggshell. You will be aware of yourself doing the exercise, but will feel that your entire body can't move. This will certainly occur in our practice. There's another state: During the seated meditation you might find that your legs disappear and you can't remember where they are. You will also find that your body, arms, and hands disappear, with only your head left. As you continue meditating, you will find that even your head is gone, with only your mind—a trace of awareness— knowing that you are meditating there. You should maintain that slight awareness. It's sufficient if we can reach this state. Why? When one does the exercise in this state, one's body undergoes full transformation. This is the optimum state, so we require that you achieve this state. But you shouldn't fall asleep, lose conscious, or abandon that slight awareness. Your meditation will be in vain should you do these things, and it will be no better than sleeping and not meditating. After completing the exercise, your hands are put together in *Heshi* and you come out of *ding*. The exercise is then done.

Appendix I

Requirements for Falun Dafa Assistance Centers

I.   All local Falun Dafa Assistance Centers are civic organizations for genuine cultivation practice, are only for organizing and assisting cultivation activities, and are neither to be run as economic enterprises nor managed using the methods of administrative organizations. No money or possessions are to be kept. No activities are to be held for healing illnesses. Assistance Centers are to be managed in a loose manner.

II.   All assistants and staff of Falun Dafa Principal Assistance Centers must be genuine cultivators who practice only Falun Dafa.

III.   Falun Dafa propagation has to be guided by the essence and inner meanings of Dafa. Neither personal viewpoints nor methods of other practice ways should be promoted as the content of Dafa, or practitioners will be led into incorrect thinking.

IV.   All Principal Assistance Centers must take the lead to observe the laws and rules of their countries of residence, and they must not intervene in politics. Improving practitioners' *xinxing* is the essence of cultivation practice.

V.   All local Assistance Centers should, when possible, stay in contact with one another and exchange experiences in order to facilitate the overall improvement of all Dafa practitioners. No locality should be discriminated against. Offering salvation to humankind means making no distinctions with respect to region or race. Genuine disciples' *xinxing* should be evident everywhere. Those who practice Dafa are all disciples of the same practice.

VI.   One needs to firmly resist any conduct that undermines the inner meaning of Dafa. No disciple is allowed to promote what he sees, hears, or awakens to at his own low level as the content of Falun Dafa, and then do what's called "teaching the Fa." That's not allowed even if he wants to teach people to do kind deeds, because that's not the Fa, but merely kind words of advice for everyday people. They don't carry the power that the Fa has to save people. Anyone using

161

his or her own experience to teach the Fa is considered to be severely disrupting the Fa. When quoting my words, one has to add, "Master Li Hongzhi[62] said ..." etc.

VII.   Dafa disciples are forbidden to mix their practice with the practices of any other cultivation way (those who go awry are always these kinds of people). Whoever ignores this warning is himself responsible for any problems that occur. Pass this message on to all disciples: It is unacceptable to have in mind the ideas and mind-intent of other practices while doing our exercises. Just one, instantaneous thought is as good as pursuing things in that other way of practice. Once the practice is mixed with others, the Falun will become deformed and lose its effectiveness.

VIII.   Falun Dafa practitioners must cultivate their *xinxing*, along with performing the movements. Those who focus solely on the exercise movements but neglect *xinxing* cultivation will not be acknowledged as Falun Dafa disciples. Therefore, Dafa practitioners need to make studying the Fa and reading the books the essential part of their daily cultivation.

Li, Hongzhi

April 20, 1994

---

[62] Li, Hongzhi (lee hong-jrr)

Appendix II

Regulations for Falun Dafa Disciples
in Propagating Dafa and Teaching the Exercises

I. When promoting Dafa to the public, all Falun Dafa disciples can only use the statement, "Master Li Hongzhi states…" or "Master Li Hongzhi says…" One is absolutely forbidden to use what one experiences, sees, or knows, or to use things from other practices, as Li Hongzhi's Dafa. Otherwise, what would be promoted would not be Falun Dafa and this would be considered sabotaging Falun Dafa.

II. All Falun Dafa disciples can disseminate Dafa through book-reading sessions, group discussions, or reciting at practice sites the Fa Master Li Hongzhi has taught. No one is allowed to use the form of lecturing in an auditorium, as I have done, to teach the Fa. No one else is able to teach Dafa and they can neither comprehend my realm of thinking nor the genuine inner meaning of the Fa I teach.

III. When practitioners talk about their own ideas and understanding of Dafa in book reading sessions, group discussions, or at the practice sites, they must make it clear that it is only "their personal understanding." Mixing Dafa with "personal understanding" is not allowed, much less using one's "personal understanding" as the words of Master Li Hongzhi.

IV. When propagating Dafa and teaching the exercises, no Falun Dafa disciple is allowed to collect a fee or accept any gifts. Anyone who violates this rule is no longer a Falun Dafa disciple.

V. For no reason may a Dafa disciple use the opportunity of teaching the exercises to treat patients or heal illnesses. Otherwise, that would be the same as sabotaging Dafa.

Li Hongzhi

April 25, 1994

Appendix III

The Standards for Falun Dafa Assistants

I.   The assistants should cherish Falun Dafa, be enthusiastic to work for it, and be willing to serve others voluntarily. They should take initiative to organize exercise sessions for practitioners.

II.   The assistants need to practice cultivation in only Falun Dafa. Should they study other practice's exercises, it automatically means that they have forfeited their qualifications for being practitioners and assistants of Falun Dafa.

III.   At the practice sites, assistants must be strict with themselves but generous with others. They have to maintain their *xinxing* and be helpful and friendly.

IV.   The assistants should spread Dafa and should teach the exercises sincerely. They should actively cooperate with and support all Principal Assistance Centers' work.

V.   The assistants should teach the exercises to others voluntarily. Collecting a fee or accepting gifts is forbidden. Practitioners should not seek fame or profit, but merit and virtue.

Li Hongzhi

Appendix IV

Notification for Practitioners of Falun Dafa

I.   Falun Dafa is a cultivation way of the Buddha School. No one is allowed to propagate any religions under the guise of practicing Falun Dafa.

II.   All Falun Dafa practitioners must strictly observe the laws of their countries of residence. Any conduct that violates a country's policies or regulations would directly oppose the merits and virtues of Falun Dafa. The individual concerned is responsible for the violation and all of its consequences.

III.   All Falun Dafa practitioners should actively uphold the unity of the world of cultivation, doing their share for the development of humankind's traditional cultures.

IV.   Students—both assistants and disciples—of Falun Dafa are forbidden to treat patients without approval from the founder and master of Falun Dafa, or without obtaining permission from appropriate authorities. Furthermore, no one is allowed to accept money or gifts for healing illnesses of one's own accord.

V.   Students of Falun Dafa should take cultivation of *xinxing* as the essence of our practice. They are absolutely not allowed to interfere with a country's political affairs, and moreover, they are prohibited from getting involved in any kind of political disputes or activities. Those who violate this rule are no longer Falun Dafa disciples. The individual concerned should be responsible for all consequences. A cultivator's fundamental aspiration is to progress with diligence in genuine cultivation and to reach Consummation as soon as possible.

Li Hongzhi

165

Glossary of Terms and Pronunciation

Arhat – enlightened being with Attainment Status in the Buddha School who is beyond the Triple World but lower than Bodhisattva.

Baihui (buy-hway) **point** – acupuncture point located at the crown of one's head.

Bodhisattva – enlightened being with Attainment Status in the Buddha School who is higher than Arhat but lower than Tathagata.

Dafa (dah-fah) – "The Great Way," or "The Great Law"; short for the practice's full name, Falun Dafa, "The Great (Cultivation) Way of the Law Wheel.

dan (dahn) – an energy cluster which forms in the bodies of some cultivators in internal alchemy; in external alchemy, it is referred to as the "Elixir of Immortality."

dantian (dahn-tyen) – "field of *dan*," a field located at the lower abdominal area.

Dao (dow) – "the Way" (also spelled "Tao").

Diekou Xiaofu (dyeh-ko shyow-fu) – Overlap the Hands in Front of the Lower Abdomen.

ding (ding) – a meditative state in which the mind is completely empty, yet aware.

eight Extra Meridians – in Chinese Medicine, these are meridians that exist in addition to the twelve Regular Meridians. Most of the eight Extra intersect with the acupuncture points of the twelve Regular, so they are not considered independent or major meridians.

Fa (fah) – "Way," "Law," or "Principles."

Falun (fah-luhn) – "Law Wheel" (see color insert).

Falun Dafa (fah-luhn dah-fah) – "The (Cultivation) Way of the Law Wheel."

Falun Gong (fah-luhn gong) – "Law Wheel Qigong." Both the names Falun Gong and Falun Dafa are used to describe this practice.

gong (gong) – "cultivation energy."

Heshi (huh-shr) – short for Shuangshou Heshi.

Jieyin (jyeh-yin) – short for Liangshou Jieyin.

karma – a black substance that results from wrongdoing.

Liangshou Jieyin (lyahng-sho jyeh-yin) – Conjoin the Hands.

Lotus Palm position – The hand position to be maintained throughout the exercises. In this position, the palms are open and the fingers are relaxed, but straight. The middle fingers bend slightly towards the centers of your palms.

Maitreya – In Buddhism, Maitreya is considered to be the name of the Buddha of the future, who will come to Earth to offer salvation after Buddha Sakyamuni.

Master – the Chinese term used here, *shifu*, is composed of two characters: one meaning "teacher," the other "father."

meridians – the network of energy channels in one's body that are thought to be conduits of *qi*. In Traditional Chinese Medicine and popular Chinese thought, illness is said to arise when *qi* is not flowing properly through these meridians, such as when *qi* is congested, blocked, travelling too fast or slow, moving in the wrong direction, etc.

qi (chee) – in Chinese thought, this substance/energy is said to assume many forms in the body and the environment. Usually translated as "vital energy," *qi* is thought to determine a person's health. "*Qi*" can also be used in a much broader sense to describe substances that are invisible and amorphous, such as air, odor, anger, etc.

qigong (chee-gong) – a general name for certain practices that cultivate the human body. In recent decades, *qigong* exercises have been very popular in China.

samadhi – Buddhist meditation.

Sakyamuni – Buddha Sakyamuni, or "the Buddha," Siddhartha Gautama. Popularly known as the founder of Buddhism, he lived in ancient India around the 5th century B.C.

Shuangshou Heshi (shwang-show huh-shr) – Press the Hands Together in Front of the Chest.

Tathagata (tah tah-gah-tah) – enlightened being with Attainment Status in the Buddha School who is above the levels of Bodhisattva and Arhat.

Third Eye – sometimes translated as "the Celestial Eye," this term (*tianmu*) is used flexibly and can refer to the Third Eye system or a particular component of that system, such as the pineal gland.

xinxing (shin-shing) – "mind nature," or "heart nature"; "moral character."

yin (yin) and ***yang*** (yahng) – The Dao School believes that everything contains opposite forces of yin and yang which are mutually exclusive, yet interdependent, e.g. female (*yin*) vs. male (*yang*), front of the body (*yin*) vs. back of the body (*yang*).

Zhen-Shan-Ren (jhun-shahn-ren) – "Truthfulness-Benevolence-Forbearance."

List of Falun Dafa Books in English

Falun Gong

Zhuan Falun

Essentials for Further Advancement

- -

Free Instruction and Workshops Worldwide

Falun Dafa practitioners provide free instruction and workshops worldwide. Books in different languages are available on Internet for free download. For further information, please visit the following websites:

> **http://www.falundafa.org (USA)**
>
> **http://www.falundafa.ca (Canada)**
>
> **http://www.falundafa.au (Australia)**

or call toll free: **1-877-FALUN99 (North America)**